D1068068

POWER
CORRUPTED

The October Crisis and The Repression of Quebec

Edited by Abraham Rotstein

George Bain
Jean Charney
Donald Smiley
George Woodcock
George Grant
Al Purdy
Eli Mandel
James Bacque
Peter Stevens
Dave Godfrey
John O'Neil
Alan Borovoy
Abraham Rotstein
Gad Horowitz

With the compliments
of the
Canada Council

Avec les hommages
du
Conseil des Arts du Canada

Power Corrupted

James Cross

POWER
CORRUPTED

THE OCTOBER CRISIS AND
THE REPRESSION OF QUEBEC

EDITED BY ABRAHAM ROTSTEIN

FOR

THE CANADIAN FORUM

new press Toronto 1971

ISBN 0-88770-085-3 paper

971.06
P887
F
1034.2
.P6

Illustrations/John Richmond

Cover Photo/Toronto Star

Printed and bound in Canada

new press
(Editorial Office)   (Order Office)
84 Sussex Ave.   553 Richmond St. W.
Toronto 179   Toronto 553

CONTENTS

erre Vallières

Introduction

There are a few of us left in the country who remain appalled and sickened by our government's response to the recent crisis in Quebec. Mr. Trudeau has gained unprecedented political support from both the populace and the media for the dramatic gestures of force as wielded by Parliament, the army and the police. Gestures they were, for we have yet to see what was achieved. It was conventional if belated police work that discovered the hiding place of the kidnappers of James Cross and turned up the suspected murderers of Pierre Laporte. For the rest, we have yet to be told what several thousand raids and over 400 arrests accomplished. We have yet to be told why. Ghosts of conspiracies still haunt this venture in political theatre.

What we gained vicariously in symbolic gratification, and whatever political objectives Mr. Trudeau has thereby fostered, carry with them a large price-tag over the long term.

We have devoted this book to revisiting the crisis and its long-term implications. Each of the authors brings his own lights to bear on these events. George Bain and Ann Charney recall the crisis as seen from Ottawa and Montreal respectively. Donald Smiley, George Woodcock and George Grant deal with long-term political perspectives. Dave Godfrey and John O'Neill come to grips in their different ways with the general problem of violence: Godfrey in the realm of the personal imagination, O'Neill as a broad reflective commentary on Hannah Arendt's classic essay 'On Violence'. Alan Borovoy confronts the issue of a return to normalcy and to civil liberties, arguing that the challenge presented by violence requires not a contraction but an expansion of civil liberties. Conclusions are provided by Gad Horowitz and Abraham Rotstein. Also included is poetry by Peter Stevens, James Bacque, Eli Mandel and Al Purdy. John Richmond provided the artwork.

Jerome
Choquette

richmond

The decision to select only English-Canadian authors was made deliberately. We need to begin a new dialogue between French and English Canadians in the light of recent events, but both sides must first rethink their positions. This is the central message of the article by Abraham Rotstein. This article has also been published in the special 60th anniversary issue of Le Devoir on December 30, 1970. It drew the following comment in the same issue by the editor, Claude Ryan:

"The view that Quebec is increasingly certain of forming a distinct nation will frighten those in English Canada who are only just coming around, fifty years too late, to the noble vision which Henry Bourassa once put forward — the *vision of a Canada based on 'the equality of the two races'. The idea has, on the other hand, been sympathetically received by a new generation of English Canadians, painfully aware they will be unable themselves to survive as a people, unless they rely on a nationalism more vigorous and original than that of the inheritors of what might be called an imperial tradition.*

The deceiving search for an abstract Canadian Dream has until now only served the political and economic interests of the English-Canadian bourgeoisie, and the vanity of a class of French-Canadian political function-aries. This search (for a Canadian Dream) will in the future be less and less accepted as a rallying point by those among our English Canadian fellow-citizens who aspire to a truly human society in Canada: those of us who have kept up contacts with the students in the English-Canadian uni-versities, know that these same students go more and more reluctantly for the bait of visions of goodwill coming out of Quebec.

So, as a reading of Abraham Rotstein's article will make clear, a new national consciousness is being moulded in English Canada. Insofar as this consciousness succeeds in defining itself, it will have to take account of the distinct reality constituted by the 'French-speaking nation' centred on Quebec; it will ask for the same amount of freedom and room for manoeuvre for that nation as it demands for itself.

The birth of this new English-Canadian nationalism allows one to hope that before long a genuine encounter will take place, on a footing of brotherhood and equality, between the two nations who together make up this country. From such a meeting could come the political institutions which will embody the new insight the two nations now have, into themselves and one another, as each strives to 'realize itself' in Canada."

The Editorial Board
The Canadian Forum

POSTSCRIPT

The January issue of *The Canadian Forum* containing the present articles sold out immediately on reaching the news-stands and produced a wide response in both the English and French press. This led us to think that the issue should be made available in permanent form for a wider audience.

Since the issue appeared, events have moved forward in both English and French Canada. The skepticism about the War Measures Act and its successor has grown. Further reflection and re-evaluation have given rise to some second thoughts about the Crisis, and the original perspectives of some of our authors may now command increased attention.

On the political scene, the October Crisis has initiated a new round of responses within one portion of the Canadian political spectrum.

We refer to James Laxer's formula on Quebec which has been adopted by the Quebec wing of the N.D.P. and has produced an alliance between that group and the Waffle. This became the subject of a major debate by the five N.D.P. leadership candidates in their trek across the country.

The heart of the new formula is that Quebec has the absolute right to self-determination up to and including independence.

The full significance of the formula is elusive. It originally came to us, couched in the language of socialism and as part of the Waffle program for the N.D.P. convention. But the formula has little to do with socialism as such and the outer covering fell away quickly.

In Quebec this new approach received wide endorsation and seemed to strike some responsive hidden chord in the province. Some commentators reacted by suggesting that if the resolution were approved, then Quebec would likely not go all the way to separation from Canada. An acceptable relationship could be envisaged on a fundamentally new basis. This did not seem like a cunning political move; there was something entirely genuine that surrounded this prognosis.

Robert Lemieux

The notion of "give us the right to independence, and we will likely not use it," is peculiar and unprecedented. It would be difficult to find a single independence movement anywhere that phrased its position in quite this way. Not Ireland, not the new states of Africa, not the Flemish or the Welsh.

Some hidden symbolism surely surrounded this issue and we were hard put to find it. The *symbolic* right to independence seemed absolutely crucial. English Canada was being tested for something . . . If we failed the test, the major thrust in Quebec might revert to a clear demand for outright independence. Claude Ryan stated recently that the issue teetered at the half-way point—the possibility of Quebec separation, in his view, was given a 50% chance.

Leaving aside the tactical political issue as it comes up internally within the N.D.P., is this new formulation simply a Machiavellian gesture, an inching along of separatism, or does it carry instead a hidden plea? If so, what is that plea?

Perhaps the issue runs deeper than appears on the surface. The moral burden of the past for Quebec, sits as a shadow cast on its history—the constriction of its inner sense of freedom, the spiritual albatross dragging down its growth and its vision of the future. It originates, in my view, with nothing less than the fatal formative moment when the die was cast in Quebec's future relation to English Canada. In one word, what the new formula pleads for is the symbolic liquidation of the Conquest of 1759—the spiritual release from the permanent burden of its history as a conquered people.

Nothing less, in our view, is at stake. A united Canada has a chance of surviving only if English and French Canadians begin again: begin from a point of symbolic separation and come together in the full freedom and genuine equality of the two nations. It is a superior moral basis for a new Confederation.

Abraham Rotstein
April, 1971

The Makings of a Crisis

George Bain

George Bain is married with one son Christopher. He joined The Globe and Mail October 1945 after being a Bomber pilot for four years in World War II. He gained extensive reporting experience in Toronto before being assigned to Ottawa as parliamentary correspondent and columnist.

In August 1957 he was posted to London as Globe and Mail correspondent for four years. For the next four years he was in Washington where he continued to report on the political scene. In 1964 he returned to Ottawa for The Globe and Mail. In 1964 his book *I've Been Around and Around* was published and in 1965 he won the Stephen Leacock Memorial Award for humour with his book *Nursery Rhymes to be Read Aloud by Young Parents with Old Children.* Mr. Bain's column appears five mornings a week on the editorial page of The Globe and Mail.

The makings of a crisis

GEORGE   BAIN

Shortly before eight o'clock on the morning of October 5, a Monday, a black taxi with a Lasalle cab light on it came up the one-way drive into Redpath Crescent, a quiet street of big homes that winds up Mount Royal. It stopped outside a three-story grey house with a slate roof and two men got out, one of them carrying a parcel in bright gift wrappings.

They climbed the 40-odd steps from the street, rang the doorbell, and, when the maid came, said they had a parcel to deliver for which they would need a receipt. The maid had no pencil and, as she hesitated, they pushed their way in.

They found the man they were looking for in the bedroom, getting dressed. They told him and his wife, Barbara – or so the police said later – that they were members of the Front de Libération du Québec. They put handcuffs on him and led him, now dressed in a checked sports jacket and slacks, down to a waiting cab, which then drove off in the direction of downtown.

The kidnapping of James Cross, 49, the United Kingdom trade commissioner in Montreal, was the twelfth kidnapping of a diplomat in the Western Hemisphere since this form of terrorist action began to be used in early September, 1969. All the rest had been in Latin America, and, until they heard or read about the disappearance of James Cross, most Canadians were content to believe that such things do not happen here.

*   *   *

That is one place to begin the story of what has come to be called The Crisis and of the political actions which flowed from it. There are others.

While the kidnapping of Jasper Cross as he was called, was the first act, there were earlier warnings of what might happen. These caused little public stir and, apparently, in light of later events, little enough within security forces, municipal, provincial or federal.

Three months earlier, on June 21, police were led on an informer's tip to a rented cottage at Prévost, 30 miles north of Montreal. They went under the authority of the Quebec Fire Investigations Act – the scope of which is interesting in light of later events – and staked the place out, thicker than the trees around, according to one informant.

Their most interesting find, along with four men · and two women, was a small store of leaflets, about 150 of them, which said that Harrison Burgess, the United States Consul-General in Montreal, was not just *going* to be kidnapped, but had been. The leaflets had been prepared in advance of a kidnapping apparently planned for the July 4 weekend, and they set out the terms for his ransom – terms which, in most respects, were identical with those laid down later in the Cross case.

The four men taken at the Prévost cottage were sentenced each to 15 days for contempt of court when they refused to testify about 12 bombing incidents – this at a public hearing conducted by the Quebec Fire Commissioner.

One man (later picked up again in the roundup following proclamation of the War Measures Act) was released after his 15 days, as the women already had been. The other three, after preliminary hearings, were ordered to stand trial on 44 charges, including charges of participating in a plot to kidnap the u.s. Consul-General. These charges still had not been disposed of at the time James Cross was abducted.

Still earlier, other evidence of a scheme to kidnap a foreign diplomat in Montreal was turned up – by accident. On February 26, police in a patrol car cruising in the East End of Montreal decided they should investigate – no special reason – a panel truck which had gone by. It was a rented truck. In it, the police found a sawed-off shotgun, a large wicker basket which had been sold as a child's toy-chest (but which was big enough to be used to transport a man), and, in the pocket of one man, Jacques Lanctot, one of James Cross's kidnappers, a press release which said that Moshe Golan, 32, the Israeli trade consul in Montreal, had just been kidnapped.

The two occupants of the truck were charged in the beginning with possession of an illegal weapon – the shotgun – and were released on bail. In late March, when it was decided that they should be charged with conspiracy to kidnap, one of the men was not to be found. The other, ordered to stand trial on the conspiracy charge, subsequently got bail and also disappeared. (He presented himself again, with a lawyer, in mid-summer, and, so far as is known, is in custody).

So the story could start with either of these events, which obviously were in the background to the Cross kidnapping; there was an evident intention on the part of some people – whether the same or different – to kidnap someone, preferably a diplomat. Or one could go back a full year to October, 1969, when Lucien Saulnier, the Chairman of the Executive Committee of the City of Montreal, decided to make public certain apprehensions, which, on November 27, he summarized as follows to a Parliamentary committee in Ottawa:

We now know that in Canada, individuals and groups are working actively to implement a plan which will carry the destruction of freedom, of our form of democratic government, and, in this plan, the people's will, as expressed in the ballot box, is excluded.

These individuals and groups are inspired and financed, in many cases, by foreign political powers related to an International that does not share our notion of man's fundamental liberties.

Mr. Saulnier's remarks to the Standing Committee on Broadcasting, Films and Assistance to the Arts related primarily to the Company of Young Canadians, which was the subject of the committee's particular concern. But Mr. Saulnier's concern did not stop there. Although he felt that the CYC had been infiltrated and was being used, the company was but one factor in a situation, which he believed to be revolutionary. He demanded a Royal Commission of inquiry.

Mr. Saulnier's assertions raised some eyebrows – he was looked upon as alarmist – but not much else.

One could start, as well, in 1963, when the Front de Libération du Québec first burst upon the Quebec scene with bombings and other terrorist acts, or even, in light of Prime Minister Pierre Trudeau's having said that he acted upon the sum of his knowledge of Quebec affairs as gathered from the age of three, in 1922.

That would make a long reconstruction. However, some reflection of that knowledge, as it may relate to the events of October and November, may be obtained from an article which he wrote in Cité Libre in May, 1964:

The fact is that at bottom the Separatists despair of ever being able to convince the public of the rightness of their ideas. . . So they want to abolish freedom and impose a dictatorship of the minority. They are in sole possession of the truth, so others need only get into line. And when things don't go fast enough they take to illegality and violence. . .

The future Prime Minister went on to say:

In the Province of Quebec the Jehovah's Witnesses and the Communists, two tiny minorities, have been mocked, persecuted, hated by our entire society; but they have managed by legal means to fight Church, government, nation, police and public opinion. Union men, in spite of being kicked out of their jobs for union activity, have never thought to destroy personal freedom but, on the contrary, have always made themselves its defenders, as also champions of democracy.

But our nationalists – of whom the 'experts' claim there is one dozing in the heart of every French Canadian – they despair of ever legally getting their 'message' accepted by a majority of French Canadians. They cry persecution to justify going underground as fugitives from reality.

This perhaps is not very instructive, except as it may suggest the author's belief that, dozing in the heart of every Péquist, there is an FLQ kidnapper and bomber – in which case, his own inner justification for using extraordinary measures, on the grounds of fighting fire with fire, would become very much stronger.

* * *

While shocked, both Quebec City and Ottawa reacted in a cool and controlled way, hard to recall now, to the kidnapping of James Cross. Robert Bourassa was going off on a visit to New York and Boston to reassure prospective investors about the stability of his Province – and went. Prime Minister Trudeau was still going on an official visit to the Soviet Union, which only later was cancelled.

Ottawa set up an operations centre in the East Block of the Parliament Buildings – since it was a foreign diplomat who had been kidnapped, External Affairs Minister Mitchell Sharp was the Minister primarily concerned – and from there, the House of Commons, and elsewhere, came statements which were at best equivocal on the question of negotiations. In the House on October 6, the Minister said:

Clearly, these are wholly unreasonable demands and the authors could not have expected them to be accepted. I need hardly say that this set of demands will not be met. I continue, however, to hope that some basis can be found for Mr. Cross's safe return. Indeed, I hope the abductors will find a way to establish communications to achieve this. . .

He also said, outside the House, that "it may be there are conditions that we could meet."

The main demands were for payment of a voluntary tax (the term used by the kidnappers) of $500,000 in gold bars; the release of a certain number of so-called political prisoners, eventually established to be 23; the publication in full of an FLQ manifesto, and the publication of the name and photograph of the man or woman who had led the police to the Prevost cottage on June 21. The prisoners and the gold bars were to be put aboard a chartered aircraft at Dorval in full view of television and still cameras.

Premier Bourassa, too, said, after what he called "real consultation" between the two governments, that it had been decided that the full set of demands was unacceptable, and he suggested that if they were looked at one by one, the reason why would be evident. Whether or not the two governments at this point were playing for time in the hope that the police would turn up the kidnappers – a wildly unreal hope, as later events proved – their joint public position was not one of apparent unyieldingness.

Almost at once, Canadians, who had never heard of him, became aware of Robert Lemieux, a bemoustached young lawyer, a McGill graduate and sometime defender of FLQ members in the courts, who blossomed as the spokesman for the FLQ and the imprisoned terrorists. Montreal French-language radio stations, and especially CKLM and CKAC, were directed by phone calls to trash-baskets and other places where they would find so-called communiques from the FLQ. As demanded by the kidnappers, the French-language network of the CBC broadcast the FLQ manifesto – as a private radio station already had done. And by the end of the week,

7

the story was slipping down into the body of the day's news for lack of new developments to report.

At six o'clock Saturday night, Pierre Laporte, the Quebec Minister of Labour and Immigration, was kidnapped off the street in front of his home on Robitaille street in the Montreal suburb of St. Lambert. He was taken by two masked men in a blue 1968 Chevrolet bearing licence No. J-2420. A week later he was found in the trunk of the same car outside some unused buildings at the old St. Hubert airfield.

In the welter of events of that week, what is easy to lose sight of is the fact that the War Measures Act was invoked and certain regulations promulgated, before, not after, Pierre Laporte's body was found. But that is something that belongs to a later part of this narrative.

On the Sunday after the kidnapping of his Labour Minister, who had been a candidate for the leadership against him, the 37-year-old Premier of the Province convened a Cabinet meeting under tight security in the headquarters of Hydro-Quebec in Montreal. It was reported that he would make a statement in the late afternoon, but, as it happened, he did not go on the air – speaking from a well-guarded suite on the 20th floor of the Queen Elizabeth Hotel – until three minutes to 10, in other words, until just before the first deadline given by the kidnappers, who called themselves the Chenier cell. He said in part:

> The government cannot and will not remain passive when individual well-being is threatened at its very roots. I am too proud a Quebecker not to tell you of all my resolutions and that of the government I direct to surmount this grave crisis.

He asked for public calm.

But he also spoke of its perhaps being possible to establish some mechanisms as a prelude to "discussing the application of the demands that have been made." There was a reference to the Quebec government's needing to know, as a simple precaution, that Mr. Laporte was still alive before anything else could proceed. There were some who thought the Premier was saying that he was prepared to negotiate – and one such, René Lévesque, the leader of the Parti Québecois, lost no time in saying so, perhaps with a view to making it more difficult if the Premier should change his mind.

Certainly at this point, the Premier was under agonizing

8

pressure to do whatever might be required to obtain his Minister's release. For a start, a letter had been relayed to him from Mr. Laporte which contained the awful line: "You have the power, in brief, to decide my fate." Mme. Laporte also wrote, not just the Premier but various other of her husband's colleagues – perhaps them all. It is hardly disputed any more that the Cabinet was divided, that resignations were proposed if this were done or that were not done. The pressure was not at all dissipated by the publication of a statement, signed by a weighty mixed handful of influential Quebeckers, including Mr. Lévesque and Claude Ryan, the editor of Le Devoir, saying that Mr. Bourassa's first duty was to save Mr. Laporte.

Through all of this, Prime Minister Trudeau remained in a position of what might be called low visibility, an earlier statement of his on the impossibility of doing business with blackmailers in no way compromised, not at least by any statement of his own.

On the Monday, the Quebec government, Ottawa approving, announced the appointment of a young lawyer, Robert Demers, to carry on some not-very-well-defined talks with Robert Lemieux, who had been arrested the night before for obstructing. (For one thing, the police thought he might be passing messages to the FLQ in his numerous televised press conferences).

And the troops arrived in Ottawa – 400 of them. The next day, two or three reporters caught the Prime Minister on the steps of the Parliament buildings. and Tim Ralfe of the CBC engaged him in what began as an interview and became an argument. (The CBC, which already had displayed an awesome alacrity to bow the knee when the Prime Minister said that the media were giving the terrorists too much publicity, took fright at the idea of one of its men challenging any assertion of the Prime Minister's. The broadcast was cut to shreds. This ignored the fact that Mr. Trudeau's whole style, in informal encounters especially, is to force the party on the other side to argue).

In that interview, he said, among other things, this:
I think society must take the means to prevent the emergence of a parallel power which defies the elected representatives. I think that goes any distance. So long as there is power . . . challenging the elected representatives of the people, I think that power must be stopped. It's only weak-

9

kneed bleeding hearts who aren't prepared to take these methods.

Of the presence of 400 battledressed troops in Ottawa, guarding the homes of Ministers and others, riding in their cars with them and walking with them in the streets, he said: ". . . it's more important to keep law and order in society than to be worried about weak-kneed people who don't like the looks of an army."

And finally, to the question: "How far would you be prepared to go with that?"

"Just watch me."

Mr. Trudeau in later days was to speak several times of a state of confusion which existed in the Province of Quebec, this in justification of the invocation of the War Measures Act. The confusion was by no means confined to the Province, nor was it – as the statement seemingly was intended to imply – necessarily attributable to the FLQ.

For instance: While the Prime Minister was talking of taking all steps necessary to prevent the emergence of a parallel power (a high aspiration, incidentally, for a force now estimated to number perhaps 100-150 persons), the two governments in Quebec City and Ottawa were still dabbling at the fringes of negotiation with the agents of that power, or keeping up the appearance of doing so.

In fact, while condemning the news media for giving the FLQ the publicity it desired, the government in Ottawa had already assented to one of the demands of the kidnappers, and one related precisely to publicity, namely, the reading on the French network of the manifesto.

And, while the troops were visibly on guard in Ottawa – almost too visibly on guard, as if to make the air of crisis more real and more apparent – they were not yet on guard in the Province of Quebec, where the centre of the crisis was supposed to exist; that was still to come.

And while Ottawa in the end was to insist that, in bringing in the War Measures Act, it acted at the request of, and on the strength of information supplied by, the Quebec government and the City of Montreal, the Prime Minister was already saying, "Watch me," in answer to a question about how far he was prepared to go.

✵   ✵   ✵

On the Wednesday, October 14, the Prime Minister was still going to the Soviet Union so far as anyone knew; certainly the Liberal caucus which met that day was not encouraged to think otherwise. On the Thursday, there was discussion in Cabinet about providing additional police powers, including those available under the War Measures Act, which would only require proclamation. Some Ministers hesitated about that, but that is not the point; the point is that the letters on which the government ostensibly acted – lawyer's letters as one Liberal subsequently described them in private – were still about 12 hours from being delivered from Quebec City and Montreal. And in the early hours of the morning of Friday, the War Measures Act was proclaimed.

The excuse for the proclamation of the War Measures Act was that a state of incipient insurrection existed. What this threat consisted of – other than the two kidnappings which, alarming though they were, hardly constituted an insurrection in themselves – has never really been explained. On the Saturday in the House of Commons there were allusions to much bigger plots, such as Justice Minister John Turner's:

They will stop at nothing to subvert democratic government in this country. While their prime target today may be the government of Quebec, there is every reason to assume – indeed, I think there are many clear indications – that other governments and indeed the central government of this country fall within the purview of their endeavours.

Nothing has been heard since in substantiation of that apocalyptic vision.

Jean Marchand, the Minister of Regional Economic Expansion, said that the FLQ had infiltrated every strategic place in the Province of Quebec, every place where important decisions were taken. He has since offered in support of this the arrest of a girl who was a receptionist in Premier Bourassa's outer office.

And, on Saturday night, the body of Pierre Laporte was found in the trunk of a car parked near the old St. Hubert airport. A Montreal radio station had been told where the car might be found – the same car, incidentally, as had been used in the kidnapping. The horror with which the news was received submerged very many questions which might have been asked about the use of the War Measures Act. In the House of Commons, the Conservatives, who initially were

11

torn about how they should react to the government's having invoked this extreme legislation, on the Monday summarily abandoned the amendment which they had offered during the day on Saturday which would have revoked the special powers at the end of October. After the killing of Pierre Laporte, only 16 members of the New Democratic Party voted not to approve the government's resorting to the War Measures Act; four more of that Party voted in favour and three more were absent.

As the weeks went by – the number of arrests under the War Measures Act quickly went past 400 and then dropped off – the polls showed overwhelming support for the actions of the federal government and the government of the Province of Quebec, support which Pierre Trudeau was not above crowing over. There was no widespread disposition to ask questions about the necessity of the emergency powers, or even about whether they were proving to be of any unique value.

Before the end of the year the chain of events which had begun with the kidnapping of James Cross on the morning of October 5 – or earlier – had been completed. On December 3, police and soldiers surrounded a house in North Montreal, Mr. Cross was brought out and turned over at the pre-arranged spot at the Expo site, and his kidnappers, plus the wives of two and the child of one – seven persons in all – were flown to Cuba. On December 27, three men, believed to have been the kidnappers of Pierre Laporte, were flushed out of a farmhouse where they had been hiding, 20 miles southeast of Montreal.

And, with it all, the questions remain – including whether these last results, gratifying as they might be, were in any way attributable to the special powers and whether they absolutely could not have been obtained otherwise.

And there are lots more.

For instance, to go right back to the beginning, what were the identifying marks of the apprehended insurrection in the name of which the government resorted to such extreme measures; what, other than the two kidnappings, which at the time were 12 and 7 days old, respectively, did it consist of?

And these:

Why, when it had received Mr. Saulnier's doleful tidings with so manifest a lack of interest a year earlier, did the federal government give the same evidence such weight in October? (The Prime Minister said at one point that, when the government received information from Montreal, it treated it as important – which must have surprised Mr. Saulnier, thinking back a year).

If the federal government accepted the Saulnier evidence, did that acceptance extend to the portion in which he said that revolutionary activities in many cases are inspired and financed by foreign powers – and, if so, will the government elucidate?

Does the government not owe it to itself (to leave aside the rest of us) to say much more than it has done about the whole circumstances surrounding the proclamation of the War Measures Act so as to avoid one or the other of the charges that it was inexcusably complacent before or inexplicably excited later?

What results are to be claimed for having given the country a taste of police powers usually associated with the more obscure Latin American dictatorships except that 450-odd persons were snatched out of their beds or off the streets, stuffed in jails for varying periods and, in most cases, not charged with anything?

What powers, in fact, did the police in the Province of Quebec need more than the already extensive powers available to them under the Quebec Fire Investigations Act (bombings come under fire investigations) and the Coroner's Act?

What – if the real danger was that already overworked forces, municipal and provincial, would be overwhelmed if masses of students took it into their heads to demonstrate in support of FLQ, did the regulations under the War Measures Act do that the presence of troops, acting in support of the civil power, could not?

To what extent was the danger of a divergence developing between Mr. Bourassa and Mr. Trudeau – the first tending towards negotiation to secure the release of the prisoners, and the second insisting that government could not negotiate with blackmailers and remain a credible agent of law and order – to what extent was that the real danger which the two men confronted?

And to what extent, if that was the case, was the apprehended insurrection a myth, a thing of threatening appearance

13

but no real substance, in which they could unite in confronting and to which all else, including the kidnappings, would be safely subsidiary?

And, finally, is there not some considerable merit in the suggestion of the Opposition Leader, Robert Stanfield, that a judicial inquiry should be instituted – it could take some evidence in private, if need be – so as to assure Canadians that substantial civil liberties were not put in hock for reasons other than those so inadequately stated?

From Redpath Crescent to Rue des Recollets

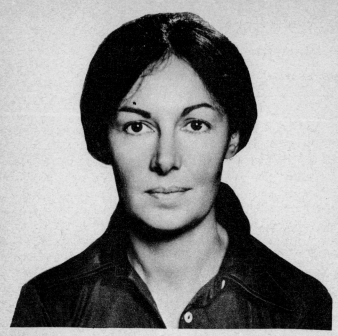

Ann Charney

Ann Charney is a Montreal freelance writer and journalist who has contributed articles on the French Canadian cultural scene to leading newspapers. She has written for the National Film Board and is currently at work on two novels. She is a graduate of McGill and the Sorbonne.

From Redpath Crescent to Rue des Recollets

ANN CHARNEY

On December 3rd, 1970, the release of James Cross seemed to bring an unexpectedly happy ending to a series of events that are credited with transforming the political climate of this country. The day Mr. Cross was released, the atmosphere in Montreal was one of relief and optimism – "the end of the sixty day nightmare" as one CBC commentator described it. The ordeal that came to an end for Mr. Cross seemed to liberate the rest of us, at least momentarily, from the sense of gloom and cynicism with which we had lived in Montreal for those past few weeks.

Unlike Mr. Cross, however, or his abductors for that matter, we continue to live with the effects of these events. A happy ending did not remove these effects, nor did it mitigate their gravity. There is no safe-conduct possible to the past, the time when we were a dull but enviable country, to whom other nations and individuals turned for aid and asylum.

The time of our innocence is irretrievably lost. It is now seven of *our* citizens who are exiles for life in a foreign country because of their political beliefs and the actions they performed in their name. Others, their compatriots, are being sought for the political murder of another Canadian, a provincial minister. An entire province has come to know life under emergency rule and the realities that go with it: armed combat troops in the streets, arrests and searches without warrant, imprisonment without charge or bail, police brutality.

As a result of all that has happened, our sense of reality has been altered. Events that were unthinkable before October 5th, which, when they did happen, were considered highly exceptional and shocking, have now passed into the image we have of ourselves, of our country, and of its citizens. Whatever happens in the future, October 5th, 1970, marked us both collectively as a people and individually in all sorts of different ways.

Yet, when it all began, few of us anticipated the impact of what had just happened, or the escalation that would follow.

On October 5th, the Cross kidnapping shared the front page with Janis Joplin's death from an overdose of drugs, and it is hard to say which incident evoked more interest. Almost immediately afterwards, however, it became clear, that for most of us in Quebec, there would be no other important news for a long time to come.

On October 6th, the seven demands of the FLQ were made public. They gave us our first hint of how extensive this affair might become. Another clue that probably went unnoticed at the time, was, that even as early as the second day of the crisis, the paranoid fantasy that was to become eventually a full blown vision, had already captured the minds of some public spokesmen and editorial writers.

On October 6th, Jean Paul Desbiens, editor of *La Presse*, and the onetime frère Untel, wrote in that newspaper that one could imagine the FLQ demanding "all sorts of other conditions, all sorts of other victims, a child perhaps. . .". We were informed by three other Montreal newspapers on the same day, that Bourassa, Trudeau, and Drapeau, are all on the list of "preferred names" for future victims. An expert on the Palestinian guerilla movement was quoted widely on his belief that the FLQ would use the "selective assassination" principle. (What do experts do between crises?)

Throughout the crisis, *La Presse* consistently followed a "hard" editorial line that was often in conflict with individual reports by its journalists. The irony here, one that often develops in Quebec, is the strange conversion that occurs in certain individuals after they come in contact with power.

Desbiens, for example, when he was the anonymous "frère Untel", was one of the first brave voices to attack the Quebec establishment of the early fifties. Gérard Pelletier, in 1965, had this to say about Quebeckers who became involved in federal politics: ". . . those who go to Ottawa, often lose, in a year or two, the common sense of Quebec. . . . only from the interior of Quebec can one understand what's happening there" (*Liberté*, v. 7, no. 3). Mr. Pelletier obviously did not

18

heed his own advice. In an open letter to him, in *Le Devoir,* December 2nd, 1970, Jean-Ethier Blais, a writer and professor, reminded Mr. Pelletier of the time when an attempt was made to remove him, because of his articles, from the editorial board of *Le Devoir.* Mr. Blais defended him at that time but now it was he who was being persecuted – his home was raided under the War Measures Act – and he wondered if Mr. Pelletier would express on his behalf the same indignation and support that he had once received. Similarly, Prime Minister Trudeau's contradictions and Jean Marchand's inconsistencies, have been so well documented lately that they need not be repeated here.

A development in the other direction, from co-operation to conflict, can also be found. Thus Michel Chartrand was Drapeau's campaign manager in 1945, and Pierre Vallières, in 1963, was made editor of *Cité Libre,* on Trudeau's departure from the magazine.

To return to initial indications of what were to become the main themes of the crisis, we find that the tendency to encourage fear and panic from the outset, was accompanied by an inclination on the part of the federal government to use the kidnapping as a way of confronting the real opposition in Quebec, that is, the wide spectrum of political, economic and social groups united through their belief in an independent Quebec.

In his first public statement on the C.B.C., Mitchell Sharp informed us that the kidnapping would certainly hurt the separatist cause. For the uninformed, it was only a simple step to conclude from this that separatists, FLQ sympathizers, and active terrorists were probably all tied in. At the least, this kind of statement confirmed the prejudices that nationalists already had about each other and thus drove them further apart.

It was also apparent from the outset that the FLQ action while it shocked most people, appealed to an indeterminate number, on all sorts of levels. One of these, hardly recognized, was the level at which people respond passionately to symbols that are meaningful to them.

On October 7th, most of the newspapers in Quebec reproduced facsimiles of the FLQ communiques. These carried the now familiar emblem of the habitant-patriot, armed with a gun, and the three colours of the flag of the patriots of 1837. The November issue of *Actualité,* devoted to the crisis, pointed out that some of the FLQ demands and its manifesto represented a very astute choice of valid and urgent Quebec issues. Similarly, the symbolism of the movement linked it to the long history of Quebec's alienation from the rest of Canada, and, in particular, to the greatest humiliation that the nationalist sentiment had ever encountered historically, the defeat and executions of 1837.

Many Quebeckers have become reacquainted with that tragic uprising through a recent "underground" history of Quebec, *Petit Manuel d'histoire du Quebec,* by Leandre Bergeron. Directed at a mass audience, it aims to "reclaim our history, the first step in repossessing ourselves, and then, our future." It is certainly significant, that a history as revolutionary as this one, was, on November 28th, number 1 on the best seller list in Quebec.

Whatever feelings they had about the FLQ and its methods, many French Quebeckers could not help feeling some thrill as the humbled flag of a suppressed revolt was resuscitated and splashed across the pages of every newspaper in Canada. In the same way, the names of the FLQ cells, and the language of their communiques, emphasized many aspects of the past, which traditional histories had intentionally left out. The extent of such re-awakened pride is hard to gauge. There was no organized, official way, in which it could express itself at that time. Indications of it, however, were frequently evident in conversations with friends and neighbours.

More concrete support became evident from the time that the FLQ manifesto was broadcast. For most people in Quebec, bombings and kidnappings remained mad and dangerous acts which they would never support, but, at the same time, a certain number of these people could not help recognizing that the injustices listed in the manifesto were very much like those they themselves had suffered, and which, for the most part, were overlooked by the society in which they occurred.

It is interesting that of the seven FLQ demands, the one conceded by the government was the broadcasting of the manifesto. Through it, the FLQ succeeded in giving the public a quick course on politics through total immersion. One wonders why Marshall McLuhan wasn't advising Trudeau this time.

If one reads it objectively, one has to admit that the manifesto is written simply, and the grievances it enumerates are often real. Its emphasis, throughout, is on social and economic issues rather than on independence. Most significantly, the manifesto names names; instead of the usual revolutionary jargon that abstracts reality to fit into a universal scheme, these accusations are very specific. They range from Noranda Mines to The Iron Ore Company of Canada, to the Power Corporation which owns most of the news media, to the Catholic Church, to Eaton's, St. James Street, Westmount. Even the Vaisseau D'or, the controversial restaurant owned by Mayor Drapeau, is mentioned.

Alongside the fear, the exploitation of the crisis, and the surprising support for the manifesto, a fourth tendency evident from the outset and amplified subsequently, was the extreme and generally futile policy resorted to by the police. Their impotence in capturing the real culprits led them to lash out fiercely at all those who in any way represented opposition to the established regime.

On October 8th, the third day of the crisis, *La Presse* reported that an unknown number of raids had been carried out by the police, and that some arrests had taken place. Amongst them were four members of the workers' committee in St. Henri, a working class area in Montreal, who for a time were refused access to counsel, and were held without charge. From then on, the police crusade against known sympathizers, radicals, leftists, political dissenters, and union officials, was on. On the same day, Robert Lemieux, counsel for the FLQ, accused the police of kidnapping citizens, and unlike the FLQ, not even naming them.

From then on until October 10th, each day brought further expansion of the basic themes of the crisis, but no change in context. Apart from the escalation in tension, the first five days of the crisis were very much one like the other. They stand out, in retrospect, as a special period, quite unlike any other I have ever witnessed in Montreal.

For one thing, everywhere one went, people seemed revived and animated in a way that would have been hard to imagine

21

even a week before. The weather refused to cede to the rigours of winter and it was a late, sunny fall, in which every warm day is precious because it may be the last before the inevitable snow storm. Against this background, the fatigue and suspicion that usually characterize relationships between people in big cities, gave way to a mood which, oddly enough, was reminiscent of a celebration. In public places such as the Metro people talked with an intensity that was unprecedented. In my own neighbourhood people spoke to each other, to shopkeepers, for the first time in years on a level other than the most superficial. We had been forced to look at each other in a way that is uncommon in ordinary times. In spite of the shock, fear and disapproval that so many felt, their expression and their gestures denied that the effect of the crisis had been all negative.

In the midst of all this intensity, little humorous quirks went almost unnoticed. The Quebec Justice Minister demanded that a letter from Cross, proof of his being alive, carry the sentence, "It is now five days since I left and I want you to know, darling, that I miss you every minute". If Mr. Choquette's imagination has been formed by pulp literature, lawyer Lemieux's on the other hand, comes straight out of the mystery genre. In protesting against this demand, he insisted that the sentence was part of a secret code that would reveal to the authorities Mr. Cross's hiding place.

On October 10th the FLQ altered the whole context of the crisis in a way that went beyond anyone's imagination. While Premier Bourassa was in New York (curious that this absence was possible while Prime Minister Trudeau felt that he had to cancel *his* trip to New York to address the United Nations), Choquette gave a negative reply to the FLQ demands. The FLQ's instantaneous answer was the abduction of a provincial cabinet minister, Pierre Laporte.

The audacity and timing of the second kidnapping caught everyone by surprise. Apart from all rational considerations, the drama and daring in this act affected many people. For the French in the poorer districts of Montreal, as they watched panic and terror spread amongst the ruling classes of Quebec, there was something of the same satisfaction that their ancestors in France must have experienced during the French Revolution. This is not to say that they were ready to participate in a revolution, or that they would have welcomed one. On the contrary, in the following week, as panic seeped down from above, they were prepared to back all repressive measures. However, in those first few days after Laporte's kidnapping, there was an undeniable feeling of support for "our boys" in certain Montreal neighbourhoods. This support should not be confounded, as it was by our leaders in Ottawa, with backing of violent actions such as kidnappings. It was rather an emotional response of passive spectators, who, for the most part, had no intention of getting into the ring.

Open, massive meetings of support for FLQ aims began to occur at the end of this, "the longest week". On Sunday night, October 11th, before an enthusiastic crowd of more than 1000 people, Paul Cliche, president of FRAP, the civic opposition party in the forthcoming election in Montreal, condemned the violence of the system and enumerated a long list of labour and political conflicts. He noted that FLQ violence was directed not against the people but against the establishment. His sentiments were seconded in the days to come by a number of different groups and organizations. Amongst them were the Laurentian and Montreal Councils of the Confederation of National Trade Unions, professors' unions, student organizations, specific departments in the University of Montreal, almost all of the University of Quebec, certain CEGEPS, and newspapers such as *Québec-Presse*.

In the midst of these manifestations of support came the first wave of the right wing backlash. Lawyer Lemieux was threatened by a group who called themselves The Canadian Vigilantes, and who informed him that if anything happened to Cross "we shall come and slaughter you and yours. This is no joke." Another instant lunatic group, Mouvement de la Justice du Québec, began leaving communiques, like the FLQ, to be retrieved by the police. In one of them, found in Place Bonaventure, they gave warning that if Cross was harmed, they would avenge him by the death of three members of the family of one of the political prisoners. Finally a third group, Le Front de Libération Chrétien, did not go as far as threats but condemned the FLQ as "traitors to their race".

Right wing conservative sentiments were not only expressed by extreme groups. In the face of student-union-intelligentsia support of FLQ aims, strong reactions of disapproval came forth from the bourgeoisie, petite and otherwise, and its elected representatives.

In the midst of this kind of polarization and indecision, the Quebec government reacted with total ambiguity.

On Sunday, October 11th, it was announced that in the evening Premier Bourassa would state the government's position on the new FLQ kidnapping. The audience that awaited the Premier's decision was, in terms of size and alertness, the ideal captive audience. Unfortunately, the statement when it was finally read, managed to confuse just about everybody. It was so ambiguous that hardly anyone agreed on what had been said. Radio-Canada decided immediately that the answer was no to negotiations, but an hour afterwards, a panel of journalists disputed this interpretation. English CBC called it a "firm no". They remained with that interpretation after Radio Canada's reversal, and in spite of the public apology of Gilles Derome, the reporter who had given the first interpretation. One wonders whether the CBC and Radio-Canada ever listen to each other. The next morning, *Le Devoir* called the incident a "monumental blunder".

The population, left without clear direction, sought for the most part to resolve the issue personally, at least in their own minds. The desire for news was insatiable. Everywhere one went, radios blared, repeating over and over the same facts or suppositions, and yet it seemed that one couldn't get enough information. In between news bulletins, people argued and talked, seeking through consensus to solidify their own particular point of view. Hot lines had never been so popular and their audiences were no longer composed only of the lost, the lonely and the bored. People who would have found it inconceivable a month before, now listened attentively to "the people", and repeated their opinions, hoping to find magic solutions.

Towards Tuesday it appeared that the government had opted for negotiation. Robert Lemieux had been arrested earlier in the week, and for a while it seemed that even the provincial government would have difficulty in obtaining his release from the Police. The first meeting between him and the government-appointed mediator, Robert Demers, took place in Lemieux's prison cell, but Tuesday he was finally freed and negotiations proceeded. While these meetings were going on in a general atmosphere of optimism, armed combat troops were moved into Ottawa.

Ostensibly, there seemed to be no conflict between Ottawa and Quebec at this time, but the troops in Ottawa were in fact an early indication that the negotiations were, for the government, a stalling device. Another discordant note from the outside came from Premier Robarts, who said that the Quebec situation had evolved into a total war and the time had come to stand and fight.

In Quebec, on the contrary, the mood was one of conciliation and optimism. On Wednesday, October 14th, a group of French-Canadian moderates, including both René Lévesque and Claude Ryan, and all of Quebec's top labour leaders, attacked Trudeau's expressed contempt for the "bleeding hearts" of democracy, repudiated Premier Robarts' statement, and urged the government to save the lives of the two hostages, and thus affirm that individuals were more important than institutions, and not vice-versa. They also criticised "certain outside attitudes . . . which add to an atmosphere that has already taken on military overtones – (a situation) which can be blamed on Ottawa". Similarly, a group of influential middle-class Quebeckers, calling themselves the "Friends of Pierre Laporte", demanded that negotiations be made solely by the Quebec government without interference from Ottawa. On the 16th of October, *Le Devoir* carried testimony from a wide variety of citizens who gave their support to the Ryan-Lévesque position.

Tragically, as so often before in the history of Quebec, its elected leaders saw this popular movement as a personal threat rather than as a potential vehicle for unity and social change. Negotiations were broken off abruptly, and the army was called in. On October 16th The War Measures Act was proclaimed, and the witch hunt was on in Quebec.

Overnight Montreal changed. If ever there had been some illusion of unity between the English and French in Montreal, on Friday the protective screen crumbled and the gulf was there for all to see. Walking the streets of the city, talking to people, reading the newspapers, it was possible at last to understand the indifference which in other places and at other times we had all found so shocking.

Like the "Aryan" Germans of the 1930's, the English in Montreal, saw no anomaly in carrying on their lives as usual while a significant number of their fellow citizens lived in fear of the midnight knock on the door. The rationale was of course, that if they were innocent, they had nothing to fear. But the complacency of the English was not borne out. We now know that the majority of those arrested were released without being charged with any offence. Inevitable victims of a crisis? Perhaps. Amongst them, however, there were almost no English sacrificial lambs.

It is easy to understand the silence of the English community, even its righteousness. For the most part they had never attempted to understand what the others wanted, nor why they wanted it, and now their fears and frustrations were easily played upon by their leaders.

In his speech to the nation on Friday evening, Prime Minister Trudeau warned his audience that the next victim of the terrorists could be a "manager of a caisse populaire, a farmer, or a child." Jean Marchand assured us solemnly that the FLQ had "thousands of guns and rifles and machine guns in its hands, bombs, and enough dynamite – at least 2000 pounds – to blow up the heart of Montreal. FLQ members had infiltrated vital institutions in Quebec, holding key posts and taking important decisions". He was also cited by *Le Devoir* as saying that if measures had not been taken, in a month or a year the separation of Quebec would have become a reality.

While the English community relaxed into their familiar state of false security, forged once again out of fear, a large segment of the French met amongst themselves, counted their victims, and exchanged the bits of information and rumour that were inevitable in a community where everyone knew someone who had been arrested or had their house raided.

As a result, the Quebec crisis had acquired another front: apart from the power confrontation between the FLQ and the government, there was now direct and indirect confrontation between the government and all those in the wide spectrum of dissension who did not approve its decisions or actions. This led to a further Quebec-Ottawa, English-French polarization. *Québec-Presse* put it in the simplest terms: the army was in Quebec not to protect the people but the rulers; there were no police or soldiers guarding homes in the east end of Montreal. In Westmount, however, as Peter Desbarats commented on his TV program "Hourglass", the latest status symbol was a soldier on the front lawn.

With time, perhaps, the suspension of civil liberties, the arrests and searches, might have evoked some indignation as well as some sympathy for those who were its victims. The shock that followed the death of Pierre Laporte, however, drowned out all other sentiments and made the expression of any reservations about the War Measures Act, almost suicidal.

Silence and polarization became the order of the day. The few brave souls who dared to question the alleged size of the FLQ conspiracy, those who made a distinction between conspiracy and dissension, those who pointed out certain inconsistencies in the government line, these individuals were treated as inhuman aberrations who advocated treason and disrespect for the dead. It is still amazing to me how widespread and emotional this reaction was and is. Over and over again, calm, reasonable, intelligent people were aroused to the point of violence by the slightest suggestion of criticism. The death of Pierre Laporte had converted us overnight from a seemingly blandly democratic people, into a nation of fanatics bent on blind revenge.

The death of Laporte was a monstrous event. The Kennedy and Oswald murders altered irrevocably the sensibility of a generation that witnessed them – in the form of the inevitable spectacle. The discovery of Pierre Laporte's body had something of the same horror about it, a horror that was both real and theatrical as we, the radio audience, waited in suspense, for the pliers to open the trunk of a car and reveal its contents. The reporter who kept us informed on the progress of this operation, felt obliged, for some strange reason, to remind us that this was an exclusive report and that he was the only outsider on the scene. Then, when the trunk was finally opened, revealing the body of a man, he assured us that he knew the identity of the corpse, but he could not divulge it. The grotesque overtones of that night were repeated by the coroner on television, who, while giving his report of the autopsy, mimed the gestures of a strangler who used a chain to do his work.

Pierre Laporte's funeral, under security measures such as this city has never experienced before, was the point at which the tension of the last few days became, at last, intolerable. Some reflex of self-preservation cut the intensity of the link that had been forged between people and events. The crisis was by no means over. Neither then nor now. For a great majority, however, totally drained of all spontaneous reaction, taxed beyond their usual emotional capacity, what was to happen subsequently, was no longer a matter of interest or concern.

Some of the events that followed were in themselves quite dramatic and provocative: the discovery of the house where Laporte was held and eventually killed; the smearing of FRAP; the municipal election; the affair of the "provisional government"; the inquest into Laporte's death; the continuing repression and harassment; the new watchdog policy towards teachers and journalists; the proposed identity cards for one part of the country; the admitted mistreatment and beatings of prisoners. For most people, (those not directly affected), these events were like the reverberation of a storm that had passed. All they wanted now, was a return to "normal", at any price.

The happy conclusion of the Cross kidnapping seems to have restored this condition to our society. This, at any rate, is the way English Canadians would like to see it. Premier Robarts, who saw Quebec on the edge of total civil war in the midst of the crisis, told us a few weeks later, on December 5th, "I believe Canadians are drawing together as they have not for many years in a deeply held desire to maintain a distinct Canadian identity and to strengthen that which we hold dear in Canada." Premier Robarts certainly spoke for the majority of Canadians, but to what extent his "we" includes French Quebec, is another matter. Another current attitude which may also be questioned, is one which rationalizes the extreme measures taken by the government in coping with the Quebec crisis as necessary for, what it is hoped will be, the final eradication of Canada's long standing malignancy – Quebec nationalism.

The situation is not unlike the one after the last provincial election, when the Bourassa victory was celebrated by the English community in Quebec as the beginning of a new era of unity and security. We know now how long that lasted. It is only a question of time before this new state of false security is shattered, in its turn.

The division between French Quebec and the rest of Canada has never been so great. At its origin there are social political and economic inequities, but more crucial than these, and harder to correct, there is the "humiliation" of which Claude Castonguay, the Minister of Health spoke in the Provincial Assembly. "Humiliation more than poverty," he explained is at the root of the crisis.

The reaction of the Federal Government has aggravated this ancient wound. In the face of an unprecedented challenge, it could only resort to old and tried reflexes, which, in the long run are always doomed: reinforcing police effectiveness, bringing up troops, setting up a reign of intimidation and terror for some. Whatever its motives, such a reaction instead of upholding democracy, has confirmed the image of colonialism. It is also necessary to ask, at this point, where were the defenders of democracy and civil liberties when public manifestations were banned in Montreal a year ago, thus making all mass protests illegal?

Phase one of the present crisis, which we may regard as the introductory stage, is over. We have passed from it to the next phase, a longer and more uncertain period, during which the struggle for real and effective change in our society will continue. In French Quebec, more often than not, this struggle will be linked to the fight for independence.

The public opinion polls won't help us. Up to the last minute, these malleable oracles of our new age of superstition will continue to celebrate the unanimity of our country and its longing for repressive measures. But the polls have no monopoly on truth. The past has proved that.

It is difficult to anticipate when, or in what form, change will manifest itself, during this new phase, but its direction is being determined right now by our silent collusion with a policy that answers dissension by denying its existence and its premises.

Consent, Coercion and Confederation

Donald Smiley

Donald Smiley was educated at the University of Alberta (M.A., M. Ed.) and Northwestern University (Ph. D.) He has taught at Queen's University, the University of British Columbia and is presently a Professor of Political Science at the University of Toronto. Mr. Smiley was in the Royal Canadian Artillery during World War II and served in the United Kingdom, Italy, and N.W. Europe. He has been a Consultant for the Saskatchewan Government and for the Royal Commission on Bilingualism and Biculturalism, also an Advisor to the Canadian Commissioners in Indochina. He has been the President of the Canadian Political Science Association and is the author of the *Canadian Political Nationality* and numerous monographs and articles on Canadian government.

Consent, coercion and confederation

DONALD V. SMILEY

> ATHENIAN: *Now which would be the better adjudicator? One
> who exterminated all the bad brothers and enjoined the
> better to govern themselves, or one who put the government
> into the hands of the good, but spared the lives of the
> worse and brought them to a voluntary submission to this
> government? There might be still a third degree of merit in
> an adjudicator, if we could find one, who would take in
> hand a family at variance with itself, reconcile its members
> for the future by his regulations, without the loss of a single
> life, and keep them on permanent amicable terms.*
> CLINIAS: *And this third sort would be far and away the best
> of adjudicators or lawgivers.*   PLATO, *Laws,* Book 1

Any judgement about the impact of the crises of October,
1970, on the future of the Canadian Confederation should be
advanced tentatively. It is the height of presumption to assert
what "history will say" about recent events. For history is
made not only by events but by historians, and the processes
by which contemporary occurrences assume particular kinds
of significance for the future are understood hardly at all.
Ongoing developments foreclose certain alternatives and
make new options available. However, the way in which one
formulates such options is inevitably arbitrary. The uncon-
vincing references made during the recent crisis by Mr. Trudeau and some of his colleagues to Russia in 1917 indicate
that certain major political decisions were made within an
intellectual framework of classical revolutionary theory. There
are other frameworks within which political violence may be
viewed, for example, the various reports and staff studies of
the U.S. National Commission on the Causes and Prevention
of Violence. Perhaps these latter investigations have more
to say about the Canadian situation than do the writings of
Lenin and Ché Guevara.

If we look beyond the immediate events of the October

crisis, it is clear that the parallel, if not co-ordinated strategies of Messrs. Trudeau and Bourassa are directed toward reducing Quebec nationalism to impotence by polarizing the province on federalist-nationalist lines. In defining nationalism Mr. Trudeau, since well before his entry into Liberal politics, has been willing to cast his net widely enough to include even those who would give Quebec very restricted elements of a special status within Confederation. Since becoming leader of his party, the Prime Minister has been disposed toward mobilizing sentiments not only within his province but throughout Canada against the many variants of Quebec nationalism. Similarly, Mr. Bourassa has been unwilling to make the compromises with nationalism indulged in by Mr. Lesage both as Premier and as Leader of the Opposition.

It is unlikely that Quebec nationalism can be destroyed as an important political force by the methods employed by the two Liberal governments. Certainly the electoral strength of the Parti Québécois in the provincial general election of April 1970 indicates the failure in part of the Trudeau-Bourassa strategy. In the immediate future, it seems probable that Quebec nationalism will be sustained by the adverse reaction to the situation in which the Quebec and Montreal governments appealed to Ottawa for intervention, including the deployment of military force during the October crisis and beyond.

If the Liberal strategy fails, it is possible that Quebec politics will return to relative stability with a clear change on federalist-separatist lines. In the Quebec elections of last April, all the political parties except the Union Nationale promoted such a polarization, and the equivocation and internal divisions of the U.N. on the national issue no doubt contributed heavily toward its rout. It is by no means certain that such a division within Quebec in the future will range the significant political forces behind the Liberals and P.Q. respectively. Perhaps there will be the recrudescence of some variant of conservative nationalism opposing both federalism and the reformist policies of the Parti Québécois. At any rate, recent events appear to have rendered impotent those espousing other alternatives than Trudeau-Bourassa federalism and separatism.

So long as domestic politics in Quebec are dominated by a polarization between federalism and separatist forces there is a degree of profound instability within the Canadian federal system. Under such circumstances each Quebec election becomes a kind of plebiscite on the continuance or otherwise of Confederation. Even a leadership contest or some kind of other internal struggle within one of the provincial parties has significant consequences for the country as a whole. In the other provinces there has been a long-term trend toward the mutual insulation of federal and provincial politics. But so long as the major political cleavage in Quebec is on federalist-separatist lines, there is a continuing pressure for those outside the province – including of course federal politicians – to intervene in Quebec affairs. Further, the uncertainty of Quebec's future in Confederation must inevitably inhibit long-range plans for co-ordination and co-operation in federal-provincial relations.

The most dangerous possibility arising out of the present situation is that Quebec has become so polarized as to be governable only by repression. To the extent that it is governed at all, a political community is sustained by an admixture of consent and overt coercion. The thrust of liberal democracy is to enhance the proportion of education and conditioning. But the essential genius of liberal democracy is to recognize the inevitablity and even the creativity of human conflict, to legitimize and channel such conflict and, in particular, to sustain ways through which citizens will find at least tolerable resolutions of these differences by peaceful rather than violent means. I have no competence to judge whether such circumstances will soon come to prevail in Quebec. The statements about Quebec society made during the crisis by the Minister of Regional Economic Expansion and the Mayor of Montreal are deeply alarming. Even if these statements were highly exaggerated, such judgements about instability by powerful political leaders tend to be self-fulfilling. As events unravel, the measures taken by the federal and Quebec governments in October appear to me to have been totally inappropriate responses to political terrorism alone – particularly as the Laporte kidnapping and murder seem to have been the work of demented amateurs rather than disciplined revolutionaries. Thus to the extent these measures were rational at all, they were directed not toward the FLQ but toward some breakdown – real or apprehended – in the structure of political authority within Quebec itself. As this is written, Premier Bourassa is calling for a new definition of freedom within the province and his Attorney-General requests of Ottawa the continuance of the deployment of Canadian troops and new and sterner measures to deal with crime and violence. Every indication one gets from outside Quebec leads to the conclusion that there is a profound crisis of legitimacy in that society.

The relation between the economic circumstances of Quebec and radical forms of nationalism is undoubtedly a good deal more complex than is often supposed and other Canadians can have no guarantee that acquiescence in even the very heavy demands of the province will result in stability. So long as troops are deployed in the province or maintained in readiness for such duties, the cost will be high both in financial terms and in Canada's decreasing capacity to meet international commitments or exigencies – a capacity that Mr. Trudeau and his colleagues have been disposed to reduce as a matter of policy. There has been a good deal of nonsense talked recently about the alleged relation between economic injustice and terrorism in Quebec. However, the evidence now coming from judicial proceedings in Quebec indicates that the young hoodlums of the FLQ were motivated by something other than an excess of humanitarian zeal for the poor of the province. It is more likely that progress will be made in meeting the economic injustices in Quebec if there is stability rather than violence or the threat of violence. So long as the latter situation persists, capital investment is inhibited and even more crucially the people and governments of Quebec are frustrated by conditions of civil strife from engaging in social and economic reconstruction. Perhaps too, other Canadians will soon come to resist the financial burdens of buying off revolution in Quebec. The demands for inter-regional equalization are more likely to be met when they are made – as they are made by the other provinces – in the name of justice and equity, rather than, quite literally, at gun-point. Further, by his reliance on Ottawa during the present crisis Premier Bourassa has undoubtedly dissipated much of the strength that he formerly had in dealing with the federal government. According to the very rough and direct way in which Mr. Trudeau exploits power relationships, it is probable that the heavy indebtedness incurred by Quebec in October will have to be repaid.

There are other burdens which would be imposed on the rest of Canada by an unstable Quebec, burdens which to some of us would be even heavier than the purely financial ones. Mr. Trudeau and his government are steadfastly against any form of special status for the province and so the traditional liberties of Canadians everywhere in the country have been abrogated since October 16th, although the emergency is geographically limited to Quebec. So long as the Quebec authorities are sustained by a high degree of coercion and by federal assistance in the coercion, Canadian politics will inevitably tend toward a polarization on the Quebec issue. This would be the most bitter and the most unprofitable kind of cleavage it is possible to imagine. At best, it would frustrate other kinds of divisions in English-speaking Canada on such issues as relations with the United States and economic reform. At worst, it would brutalize Canadian society outside Quebec.

More than any Prime Minister in the history of Canada, Pierre Elliott Trudeau has shaped the policies of the country to his own desires. In the past, some of his detractors have accused him of rigidity in holding to certain intellectual positions which subsequent events have made irrelevant. This charge will no longer hold. During the October crisis and beyond, Mr. Trudeau's actions and utterances have belied all of those fixed principles on which he formerly stood – the principles of individualism, rationalism and pragmatism. For individualism accords rather badly with the exercise of emergency powers. Rationalism is clearly contrary to a stance which suggests that the final test of the action of a government is the amount of public support which is forthcoming for that action. And pragmatism is based on an awareness of the mutual interpenetration of means and ends and a prudent relating of the two. It is ironic that in November there has been published a collection of Mr. Trudeau's earlier writings on power and authority. This vapid rhetoric will no doubt be regarded as profound political philosophy by the dutiful membership of the Liberal intelligentsia. But in his more serious analytical writings, Mr. Trudeau has well described both the circumstances of democracy in Quebec and the conditions under which Canadian federalism can continue. Is it too much to ask the Prime Minister to employ his remarkable powers of exploration and expression to tell us where he is taking us? The Prime Minister is unlikely to explain. When speaking of the alleged actions of Claude Ryan during the crisis, Mr. Trudeau paraphrased Lord Acton to refer to the corruptions of powerlessness. Thus, in his own view, the head of the Government of Canada has been purified by power. And from this perspective, power has its own imperatives – whether the power of docile political party, the power of overwhelming public support for repressions or, ultimately, the power of the Armed Forces of Canada. Away with reason.

Canadians outside Quebec are intermeshed in relations with that society and with the United States. In a way which I do not pretend to understand, the inter-actions between English-Canada and each of these two communities will shape its relations with the other. It may well be that both Quebec and the United States are in the process of becoming so polarized internally that neither can be governed without repression and the abrogation of traditional liberties. The root impulses of the resurgence of Canadian nationalism are not primarily economic but rather judgements or sentiments that the United States has drifted from its moorings in the ideals which we share. For more than a decade now, English-speaking Canada has reacted defensively to domestic developments within Quebec. At the most extreme, we have been subjected to a continuing propaganda that Quebec has some kind of inherent right to decide unilaterally what its relations with the rest of Canada are to be. As is the case with the United States, it is time for English-speaking Canada to reassert initiative in our reactions to these external developments. The continuing political instability and repression in Quebec might well impose such burdens on the rest of the country as to strain Confederation beyond tolerable limits.

Anarchism and Violence

George Woodcock

Born in Winnipeg in 1912, George Woodcock went to
England as a child and stayed long enough to start his
career as a writer there by publishing in the *New English
Weekly, New Verse* and other typical thirties magazines.
His first prose work of significance was *William Godwin*
(1946). He returned to Canada in 1949 and since 1959 has
edited *Canadian Literature.* He served as an academic long
enough to know that by nature he was not fitted for that
type of theatre, and now merely writes and edits. His
books include *Anarchism* and *The Crystal Spirit* (on
George Orwell), *The Writer and Politics* and *The Paradox
of Oscar Wilde*, four books of verse, a score of radio plays,
a handful of travel books, three volumes of criticism on
Canadian writers and biographies of Proudhon, Kropotkin
and Aphra Behn. With Ivan Akakumovic he wrote *The
Doukhobors*; his latest book is *Canada and the Canadians.*

Anarchism and violence

GEORGE WOODCOCK

The past should have taught me. But I suppose, just as the
New Left does not learn from history, so I do not learn always
from my own experience. The press blows the trumpets, a
few carefully chosen photographs are used to deceive, and,
so primitive and gullible is one's desire for the sensational,
that at first I am tempted to believe in the enormity of the
crisis in Montreal as the news editors and the politicians
want me to do. And this although my travels have led me
into the midst of a dozen falsely magnified crises of the same
kind; I should know better – after occasions in Lima and
Calcutta and Hong Kong and Kerala – but I react in the same
way again, go to Montreal expecting God-only-knows what
manifestations of lurking terror and threatening power, and
come back having seen no soldier in the streets and no real
evidence of fear in the faces of the people.

All this leads me to the conclusion that it is not entirely a
matter of the villainy of politicians or the mythomania of
reporters. When Trudeau and Marchand, Bourassa and Drapeau, deliberately exaggerate the perils of the situation in
Quebec, and the media fervently abet them, is it not partly
because *we* desire the crisis to appear in a large image, to
impinge symbolically on our lives, to cast upon a great external screen the broken spectres of our inner fears – perhaps in
some degree also our inner hopes? "Revolutions are the holi-
days of life," said a character in Malraux's novel, *L'Espoir*,
and it is notorious that the wars of the past resulted in an
actual quickening of the sense of life. Even among pacifists
in England, I remember, the ending of World War II brought
a feeling of anti-climax. For them too a struggle that had
given meaning to existence was ended; the dullness of peace
had returned. Have we grown tired of our mild society and
our ironic selves?

•   •   •

Undoubtedly our reaction to the Quebec kidnappings was exaggerated in the sense that, however grotesque and unacceptable these incidents may have been, they were no worse than what had been happening repeatedly over a long period in other countries, including the United States, without the fabric of society collapsing in a vast mudslide. Yet were we wrong to take it all so seriously? In some ways, I suggest, no. For, symbols or symptoms, the macabre events in Quebec were like those small and sinister signs that prelude cancer, like those flights of birds into a hushed and stagnant air which are said to foretell the coming of earthquakes.

What the reaction in word and deed to these events demonstrates, even more than the episodes themselves, is the delicate balance on which a federalist society operates, particularly when, as in the case of Canada, it has been prevented by an excess of compromising caution on the part of the constitution makers from being either a centralized state on the French or British model, or a really decentralized society like the Swiss, where the presence of the communes as a

richmond

Jacques Lanctôt

third level of authority below the cantons takes politics down to the roots and where a heavy topgrowth of power is prevented by a council system of federal authority which does not admit the emergence of figureheads. (Just as there are no peacetime generals in the Swiss armed forces.)

One wonders, indeed, what the FLQ would have done if they had been operating in a country like Switzerland where there are virtually no political heroes to threaten by kidnapping and selective assassination. Would they go after the faceless gnomes of Zurich? After the unknown colonels? The very fact that one speculates in this way suggests that a society with a low and unmythological political profile like the Swiss may better be able to contain such a crisis than a society like the Canadian which has not yet determined for itself just how much political demythification and devolution of power is necessary for a successful federalism.

Canada is in fact vulnerable precisely in proportion to its attempt to perform the geographically impossible feat of being a state like any other. The CPR is decaying as a link between people because its role as a disseminator of populations to empty landscapes is ended; the regions have grown on their own, and polycentrism is a reality waiting to be recognized by the politicians. Canada could be, but is not, the first country to realize federalism at all levels as the appropriate form of administration for a vast geographical area. When every community, from Seven Persons in Alberta up to Montreal has its own communal identity, when nationalism in the crude sense becomes irrelevant within Quebec because its counterpart will not exist in Canada as a whole, we shall be on our way to the peaceable kingdom (and let us be thankful to William Kilbourn for reminding us of it at this appropriate juncture). But how?

* * *

We need now to end sentimentalization, forget for a while the symbols of nationality and race, conceal our flags (fleur-de-lys as well as maple leaf), cool our anger, remember that poverty is the basic mark of discrimination, and give up our bourgeois and Puritanical luxury of guilt. Looking back, was there anything but self-indulgent folly in Quebec? The fact is, and we should never have tired of saying it, that the two real nations are still Disraeli's – the Rich and the Poor, and that the poor are Wasps and Indians and Eskimos and Italians and Greeks and Doukhobors as well as Québécois; the fact is also that if the French were not numerous among the rich and the powerful, it was largely the fault of their own church-dominated social system, which despised trade and industry and right at the beginning left the fur trade to the Scots; the fact is also that it was the leading French Canadian nationalist of his time, Maurice Duplessis, who sold Quebec to the Americans. The average anglophone had nothing to do with the condition of frustration in which French Canadians find themselves, and he should cease feeling the guilt which the more dangerous Quebec nationalists exploit to hide the defects in their own society. Nationalists always need scapegoats; we should at least refuse to volunteer

For Quebec nationalists *are* dangerous, like any other nationalists, first for the simple reason that nationalism is atavistic – as distinct from regionalism – because it is essentially exclusivist. How great a part the idea of *keeping out* plays in all nationalisms! Most decisive of all the exclusivisms is that of language. It is no accident that the Rose brothers should have been among the linguistic fanatics who played such a reactionary role in the notorious St. Leonard affair, when a deliberate attempt was made to terrorize non-francophone inhabitants of Quebec out of the right to education in the language they preferred.

It is equally no accident that what has angered the nationalist backwoodsmen of both Canadas most against the present federal government has been its attempt to create effective bilingualism. The true radical would surely demand acceptance not merely of two but all languages at all widely spoken in a country of many origins like Canada, and there are signs that the efforts of western ethnic movements may in the end be rewarded by more tongues than English and French being recognized officially. Totalitarians always detest a multiplicity of languages because it means a multiplicity of loyalties. The efforts of Franco to stamp out Basque and Catalan, of Mussolini to stamp out German in the South Tyrol, of Kemal Ataturk to end the use of Arabic in Turkey, were all means to build the monolithic state. Their linguistic policy alone tells us in what political company the FLQ belong.

But the linguistic exclusivism of the more extreme political separatists has another significance, since it emphasizes the extent to which francophone and anglophone Canada tend towards different ways of political thinking – those represented by their respective languages. In a literary sense Quebec cannot avoid belonging to the French tradition, and the French tradition–unlike the English–is not one of gradualism, of non-violence, of empiricism, of compromise and consensus. It is a paradoxical combination of the revolutionary and the conservative, of the radical and the authoritarian, in which Bonapartism alternates with the barricades, and Victor Hugo is symbiotically linked with Louis Napoleon. Because in English we know relatively little of that tradition, we have failed to realize that the naive misapplication of Marxist verbiage by the intellectuals of the FLQ masks the real ancestry of that movement; it derives from the Jacobins, via Babeuf and especially via Jerome Auguste Blanqui, the archetypal French conspiratorial revolutionary. It was Blanqui who invented – or perhaps developed from Buonarotti – the cell system of conspiratorial organization, and who first used the term, the dictatorship of the proletariat, which Marx later borrowed (as he made most of his numerous borrowings) without acknowledgment. At first sight, Blanquism appeared to be the diametrical opposite of Bonapartism; in its most significant aspects, however, it was Bonapartism's prodigal brother, for Blanqui and his followers were intensely patriotic and intensely nationalistic, differing from the anarchist Proudhon in deifying the national state, and Blanqui in fact – if not entirely in theory – raised up a potent and durable elite; the elite of the professional revolutionaries.

richmond

Marc Carbonneau

45

One has only to examine the actions and pronouncements of the FLQ to realize that it is in all respects neo-Blanquist, and could only have emerged in a backward French-speaking society which turned largely to a romantic France of the past for its political inspiration. The cell system, the talk of the proletariat, the intense and intolerant nationalism, the revolutionary elitism, all are there, and all of them suit the FLQ for a place in the essentially authoritarian and elitist structure of French Canadian society. Pareto's cumbrous theory of the circulation of elites may not work in all contexts; but it can be used very illuminatively in one's study of French Canadian political and social relationships. For all the groups that seek power are – in a much more organized way than in anglophone Canada – elites seeking to replace the reigning stratum, in the same way as the urban middle-class elite of the quiet revolution replaced (partly by absorption) the old landowning-clerical elite. As the anglophone economic elite declines as a visible presence in Montreal, the ruling francophone elite is strengthened, and the bitterness of competing Québecois groups is increased as a measure of their frustration. Laporte – and how symbolically significant his name might appear to those obsessed with upward liberation – was sacrificed to the struggle between elites and anti-elites within Quebec.

The incident really has little *directly* to do with the rest of Canada, but indirectly a great deal, because it does make far clearer than any previous episode the sharp contrast between the still powerful elitism of Quebec, and the growing populism of anglophone Canada, which in Quebec – if it exists at all – does so only in the crude form of Créditisme with its following among the marginal farmers.

•   •   •

When John Porter's *Vertical Mosaic* was published his charting of the Canadian elites seemed substantially correct, and eighteen months ago when I wrote *Canada and the Canadians* I still thought that Porter's findings accorded more or less with my own view of Canadian society as it actually worked. Now that book has appeared, held up more than a year through publishing delays, and I am beginning to feel that the situation it projected is already changing, and that the power wielded by the economic and political elites is becoming more restricted because of increased activity among the people in many directions, often on limited but passionately held issues whose appeal runs across the political party divisions. It is an activity which is impatient with the slow methods of parliamentary change, and which therefore manifests itself in an increased tempo of demonstrations and public meetings and in a degree of extra-political direct action (up to now mainly non-violent) to hasten the regular processes. While the usual young men on the political make hover round such movements, their general tendency is not to throw up rival elitisms, as in French Canada, but to remain a smouldering among the grassroots, capable of bursting into occasional sharp flares of protest or of action. There is a looseness and a spontaneity about what is happening in anglophone Canada which I do not see in the managed conspiratorial politics of Quebec. This popular stirring can affect the more regular currents of politics; there was a strain of populism in the western response to Trudeau, as there had been in the elevation of Diefenbaker in the 1950's. But there is no necessary connection between regular politics and populist action.

How can one reconcile these two apparently different situations in the two Canadas? Perhaps the reconciliation can come from the realization that the methods needed to make populism real in English Canada are precisely those needed to dissolve elitism in French Canada, and that these – rather than the counter-terrorism of totalitarian governmental methods – may best contain the violence that appears to have become – for a year or so, perhaps even a decade or so – a part of our way of life.

Here we must draw for inspiration and argument on the libertarian tradition so grossly slandered by Pierre Trudeau at the recent Liberal Party convention when, with a demagoguery unworthy of a political scientist who knew better than he spoke, he equated the neo-Blanquist authoritarians of the FLQ with the anarchists, which means the tradition of Kropotkin and Proudhon, of Godwin and Herbert Read. Of course, the two philosophies are diametrically opposed, and the only resemblance is that on a few occasions in the past individual anarchists have, like members of most political movements, resorted to violence. There is no necessary connection between anarchism and violence, and many anarchists are also pacifists, but all share the tradition of decentralization and devolution, the tradition of direct democracy and of the distrust of the centralized state.

Since the centralized state is a palpable impossibility in Canada, that already brings us a long step nearer to the anarchist or libertarian tradition. I do not suggest a society wholly without government is a foreseeable possibility, but I do believe that a thorough survey of the voluminous anarchist schemes of administrative, social and economic decentralization, and of the populist techniques of direct and quick democracy (particularly the greater use of the referendum, initiative and recall to give reality to political participation between elections), would enable us to get away from routine liberal thinking and to devise a political organism – rather than a political system – sensitive to urgent shifts of opinion, immediate social needs, and flexible on all levels from the village to the nation. The disadvantages of Canada from an ordinary political viewpoint – its space, its linguistic and cultural diversity – can become positive advantages if we are willing to abandon the thought of creating an efficient monolithic state and to evolve an original political framework based on the realities of our geography and our existence: based also on the demythification of our politics.

Maurice St. Pierre
Directeur, Q.P.P.

richmond

Nationalism and Rationality

George Grant

George Grant was born at Toronto in 1918. After studies at Queen's and Oxford, he joined the department of philosophy at Dalhousie University where he taught from 1947 to 1960. In 1961 he went to McMaster University, where he has been chairman of the department of religion. He is married with six children. Previous books are *Philosophy in the Mass Age, Lament for a Nation* and *Technology and Empire.*

Nationalism and rationality

GEORGE GRANT

The politics of technologized societies are an open field for demagogic tactics. Politics is the working out of public disagreement about purposes. But politics is now increasingly replaced by administration, as disagreement about purposes is legitimized away by the pervasive assumption that all which publicly matters is the achievement of technical 'rationality'. Elections become increasingly plebiscites in which the masses choose between leaders or teams who will be in charge of the administrative personnel. In plebiscites it is necessary to have leaders who can project their images through the various media, and so catch the interest of the masses who are bored with politics, except as spectacle and as the centralizing organization for technologized life. The plebiscitary situation calls forth from the privileged classes leaders who have the will to project their personalities, and as these men are increasingly the product of the modern "value-free" university, they are likely to be willing to use any means when it suits their interests. A negative example of this thesis is Mr. Nixon. It is inconceivable that he could have been elected President in 1968 without the administrative disaster of the Vietnam war which exposed the blatant failure of the Democratic personnel to provide what was wanted at the home of the empire. For all his administrative reliability and talent, he simply lacked the image for the plebiscites in comparison with his Republican predecessor or his Democratic alternatives.

In recent Canadian events there have been two successful plebiscitary leaders – Mr. Diefenbaker and Mr. Trudeau. Mr. Diefenbaker had, however, one grave disadvantage. He had certain residual loyalties (for example, to the independence of Canada) which acted against the demands of 'rationality' and administration. Therefore despite his ability to transmit his image he came into conflict with the sheer needs of the private and public corporations – that is with state capitalist 'rationality' itself. He could not continue to get votes in the parts of Canada which were most enmeshed in the continental administrative system, and where the voters were most at the mercy of the legitimizing powers of that system. But, Mr. Pearson lacked the plebiscitary appeal so that he could not get an outright majority, even although his actions were acceptable to continental administrative 'rationality'.

Mr. Trudeau combines plebiscitary appeal with acceptance of the assumptions of state capitalist 'rationality'. He must therefore be seen as a formidable figure in our public life. In his writings he has unequivocally stated that he believes the best future for French Canadians is to be integrated into the Canadian structure as a whole, and that the Canadian structure should be integrated into the whole western system (if not in an overtly political sense, at least economically and socially). Throughout his career his appeals have been to universalism, and universalism in a Canadian setting means integration into a smoothly functioning continental system. It is this union in Mr. Trudeau of charisma with the acceptance of the purposes of corporation capitalist efficiency which made Mr. Denis Smith's article about his policies so telling. The idea that Mr. Trudeau was changing our political framework from a parliamentary to a presidential system involves more than a change from Canadian to u.s. traditions. This change in political structure would fulfil the needs of a society in which administrative rule is bolstered by plebiscites about personnel.

In Mr. Trudeau's writings there is evident distaste for what was by tradition his own, and what is put up along with that distaste are universalist goods which will be capable of dissolving that tradition. Indeed this quality of being a convert to modern liberalism is one cause of his formidability. Most English-speaking liberals have lived in universalism much longer. They have not come to it out of something different, but have grown up in it as their tradition. They are apt, therefore, either to accept it automatically or even to start to be cynical about its ability to solve human problems. On the other hand, Mr. Trudeau's espousal has behind it the force of his distaste of its opposite. Recent converts are especially effective exponents of a system because they have the confidence of believing they are doing right.

Mr. Trudeau combines then administrative reliability with

the power to project his image in the plebiscites. In 1968 this image was partially a revamped Kennedy one – openness to youth and freedom, a marvellous expectation about the potentialities of our system, (no interference in the bedrooms of the nation etc.). This was effective in the Canada of Expo, especially because there was an awareness that things were not going as well in the u.s. as had been expected at the beginning of the Kennedy era. Tacitly behind this part of the image and clearly related to it, was the sense, in English-speaking Canada, that here at last was a French Canadian who would deal with Daniel Johnson and de Gaulle. Mr. Trudeau came to power by a brilliant use of television around that constitutional encounter. Indeed many of the smartest media men who now deplore his recent actions had helped him to organize that use. At its worst, Mr. Trudeau was for many English-speaking Canadian that happy phenomenon "a Frog who could deal with the Frogs". In his recent actions he has fulfilled for them that promise. As he said in October, 1970, "Just watch me".

I leave aside the intriguing question of why the Trudeau administration embarked on the War Measures Act; and I do so having taken for granted that the government had sufficient power, without its invocation, to deal firmly with what was happening in Quebec. The question then arises: does his employment of these powers make Mr. Trudeau a more or less effective plebiscitary leader in Canadian life? As far as French Canada goes, a useful answer could only be made by somebody with great knowledge of Quebec from the inside. How deep is the desire on the part of many French Canadians to exist as a Franco-American community in the midst of the homogenized English-speaking sea? Is the French-Canadian question a truly political one, in the sense that the powers of administrative rationality cannot dissolve it?

Obscurity is increased by the fact that two different voices of opposition to Mr. Trudeau seem to be coming out of Quebec. On the one hand, there is the voice of nationalism, expressed particularly by members of the élite, who care about the continuance of their community and who know that Mr. Bourassa's slogan "American technology - French culture" cannot be an adequate basis for any real survival. On the other hand are the inchoate voices of those who are the particular victims of the fact that Quebec came late into the American technological expansion – e.g. the people of east Montreal and the students who cannot get jobs. These voices seem to employ the mode of popular Marxism. What is the relation between these two forms of opposition? It has often been possible for Marxists to appear as supporters of nationalism, for example as resisters of western invasion in Russia or China. But clearly at its heart Marxism is a universalist and not a nationalist doctrine, and just as much as Mr. Trudeau's liberalism, it puts the development of technique as its priority. Also since Quebec is at the very heart geographically of the western empire, it is going to be modernized within the setting of capitalist rationality – not Marxist. Within that setting Marxism will be simply an ideology for the sympathetic, an opiate for the unfortunate. The responses of the student population will be crucial. Can enough of them

The Prime Minister proclaims the War Measures Act

be won over from their nationalism, as Mr. Trudeau has predicted, if Quebec is effectively oriented into the American system and enough managerial jobs are provided for the educated? Has capitalist rationality the means of bringing about that integration quickly enough?

In English-speaking Canada it seems that Mr. Trudeau's status will remain high. He has come through on his promise to deal strongly with separatism. That he deals with it quite outside the principles of constitutional liberties does not seem important, because although these traditions of law were the best part of the British tradition, they are not something that can hold masses of voters' minds in the age of technological rationality. Civil liberties can be a supplementary issue in times of bad employment or in connection with other failures of the system, but they cannot be a determining issue for many voters who live within modernity.

Indeed in the extreme circumstances of the War Measures Act, the two main political questions of Canadian life come together for those of us who must oppose what the Trudeau administration has done. The possibility of some freedom in the American empire is mutually interdependent with some potential 'modus vivendi' between English - speaking and French-speaking Canadians. But it is hard to move from this relation to practical judgements about immediate Canadian politics. On the one hand, it is obvious that any indigenous English-speaking Canadian society requires the help of Quebec. Yet how can this be advocated in a way that is not simply asking French-Canadians to be led along to their doom as a community? In other words are the French not best to be separatists in the face of the North American situation? This dilemma for English-speaking nationalists is even more evident because of the events of the autumn. Before these events, a certain nationalist spirit seemed to be growing in English-speaking society. This was encouraged by the obvious social failures of the United States, and also by the economic consequences of being a branch-plant society, which were coming home to many Canadians at a time of American retreat. Yet during the crisis in Quebec, a large English-speaking majority readily acquiesced in an attack not only on terrorism but on constitutional French nationalism. In the light of this, French Canadian nationalists would perhaps do well to concentrate on the possible means of their own cultural survival and to accept that English-speaking culture is only a Trojan horse for the 'rationality' of the North American monolith. What effective alliance can English-speaking nationalists offer their

French compatriots? How would it be expressed in immediate political terms? What advantage has it to offer those who seriously desire that Franco-American culture survive in a more than formal sense? Mr. Lévesque's question to English-speaking nationalists stands, and has been made more urgent by the present crisis.

Robert Bourassa

Poems

The peaceable kingdom

*(In Ottawa, after the War Measures Act
is invoked against the F.L.Q.)*

AL PURDY

Friday, Oct. 16: Along Elgin Street
traffic crawls at four o'clock
attaches with brief cases
of importance on Wellington
expensive mistresses and wives
of diplomats walking dogs
and babies in Rockcliffe Park
two Carleton students with lettered signs
VIVE le F.L.Q. on Parliament Hill
the Mounties don't lay a finger on them
below the Peace Tower
cabinet ministers interviewed on TV
inside the House
orators drone and wrangle as usual
in a way almost reassuring
In Quebec the Fifth Combat Group
from Valcartier occupies Montreal
paratroopers fly in from Edmonton
infantry from the Maritimes
And the P.M.'s comment
on bleeding hearts who dislike guns
"All I can say is go on and bleed
it's more important to keep law
    and order . . ."
All this
in the Peaceable Kingdom

Saturday, Oct. 17: No change
the two kidnapped men are still missing
In the House of Commons politicians
turn into statesmen occasionally
Reilly on CTV news demands Trudeau
    resign
Eugene Forsey does not agree
Yesterday driving into Ottawa
with my wife
citizens of no Utopia
red autumn leaves on Highway #7
–thinking of the change come over us
and by us I mean the country
our character and conception of
    ourselves
thinking of beer-drinkers in taverns
with loud ineffectual voices disagreeing
over how to escape their own limitations
men who have lost their way in cities
onetime animals trapped among the
    tall buildings
farmers stopped still in a plowed furrow
that doesn't match the other straight
    lines
as a man's life turns right or left
    from the norm
No change in the news
N.D.P. and P.C. members condemn
    the government
Créditiste Real Caouette does not
Diefenbaker thunders at the P.M.
a prophet grown old
Police raids continue in Montreal

Sunday, Oct. 18: Pierre Laporte
    found dead in a green Chev
outside St. Hubert shot in the head

hands tied behind his back murdered
A note from James Cross found in a
  church
asking police to call off the hunt for him
Crowds gather on Parliament Hill
for the same reason as myself
and stand close to the heart of things
perhaps if they were not before
have become Canadians
as if it were not beneath them
gathered here to mourn for something
we did not know was valuable
the deathbed of innocence
mocked at by foreign writers
the willingness to pretend
our illusions were real
gone now
Soon we shall have refugees escaping
  the country
expatriates of the spirit and the body
  politic
and men in prison raving about justice
defectors beyond the reach
of what we had supposed was freedom
and the easy switchers of loyalty
will change ideas and coats and countries
as they do elsewhere and are no loss
Well
I suppose these things are easy to say
and some think sadness is quite
  enjoyable
I guess it is too
but this is not an easy sadness
like my own youth full of tears and
  laughter
in tough middle age when I'm not

listening anymore sings to me sometimes
Beyond the death of Laporte
and the possible death of James Cross
the deathbed of something else
that is worth being mocked
by cynics and expatriate writers
–the quiet of falling leaves perhaps
autumn rains
long leagues of forest and the towns
tucked between hills for shelter
our own unguarded existence
we ransom day by day of our short lives
Driving west from Ottawa
we stop at a roadside park for lunch
beside a swift narrow black river
looped into calm by the park
thinking in this backwater
how the little eddy that is my life
and all our lives quickens
and bubbles break as we join
the main stream of history
with detention camps and the smell
  of blood
and valid reasons for writing great novels
in the future the past closing around
and leaving us where I never wanted
  to be
in a different country from the one
where I grew up
where love seemed nearly an affectation
but not quite
beyond the Peaceable Kingdom

ELI MANDEL

Variations on a theme
for Gilles Vigneault

my country you are a winter
like rivers of ice
the terrible knives of St. Hubert
run through the whiteness of my veins

politics pierce my heart
on the littered floor of our history
I shiver while the wardens shovel in
rag upon rag of lunatic sentences

it must be cold in the prison of quebec

and your heart
                    hurt
                              singer

through its pane
                    what do you see

icy slaves circle the river
montreal tenses against the steel of its manacles
your words drift like frozen wounds
across provincial deaths
                              blessing

a sick bride
a murderous groom
                    that wedding
whose children will be colder killers
than the words of this or any other song

le 16 octobre 1970

tonight
listening to the radio
troops take up their positions in Québec
I become French-Canadian.
            non, c'est mal entendu
I heard Trudeau
      take up his position
in French and English
        sitting in the same car
        tuning the same radio
        I had my year in France
        hearing de Gaulle
Français, Françaises
        et tout ça
et là, j'étais canadien-anglais
du côté français, écoutant
        la chute de Paris,
les étudiants dans la rue
        hors la loi
contre la loi publique.

    Et maintenant, ce soir
Au bord de la Baie Georgienne
Près du pays   de Champlain
        et tout ça
encore une fois
        j'écoute
le son de l'armée dans la rue
à minuit
dans mon village.

Who are we tonight
our British liberty revoked
à cause du FLQ,
Canadians? Canadiens?
my mind is slower than my heart tonight
freedom is like that moonlight
brisée par les vagues
de la mer douce d'autrefois
la mer qui demeure
complètement inconnue.

Mon arrière grand-père
est échappé de la France
pour y retourner
et moi, Anglo, devenu
le résultat de mon pays
an English mind
d'un coeur français
moi, je cherche
comment m'exprimer
contre cette armée.

Nous sommes nous autres
Ça ne peut pas s'expliquer
Sauf que nous demeurions les hôtes
D'un pays à tout risquer.

PETER STEVENS
Fall 1970

I   THE END OF GROWING UP

While I grew up
bombs blasted privacies of buildings:
bedrooms kitchens opened
and stairs ascended into widened air.

Houses jigsawed apart
but somehow I remained unpuzzled
nothing touched me –
a few fire bombs fell near
guns pounded at streetcorner
a city flamed across night skies.
I kept some shrapnel in a box
the school was straddled by a stick of bombs
some boys I knew were blown to pieces.

And slowly I grew up,
learning at school,
out of school trying to learn
and failing. . . .

Then, later, Canada.
I crossed its space that first year
and thought I knew it
but I've been failing up till now. . . .

The cab stands quietly purring
at the corner of the street I cross
to chase a simple ball some child has thrown
and straightening up I feel the barrel
in my back.

A sudden shuffle. . .
the cab drives me away.
The child stares after me
one arm half-raised –
a wave or ineffectual gesture of prevention –
as he dwindles in the rearview mirror.

All this time I've thought
the cards I held made a full house
and only now I realize
the easy chair I sit in is a box
that could explode
and blow the house to smithereens.
The box has let out secrets
I said I wished to know
but didn't really want to know.
Now it's far to late not to know.

I climb the stairs in darkness.
I hesitate, not knowing
if the next step's there.
An emptiness solidifies beneath my feet.
The engine of the cab I didn't know I'd called
efficiently turns over
as it waits to take me on a drive
whose end I cannot see.

II   FRENCH AND ENGLISH SPOKEN HERE
     (*an imitation of Enzensberger*) –

What am I doing here
in this country
to which by coming late
I sloughed away my past?
No longer foreign
but somehow alien here
settling into this smug province
this comfortable corner.

Where do I belong? What place
is mine on this Rapido, in this wonderland
where things get better but do not improve.
Expense accounts lead gorgeous Sheraton lives
the poor in corner stores thin as pencils
shout lead-heavy through the day-old bread,
things are getting better!
The shopping plazas separate the people

obscenity bursts out on Yonge
'cause things are getting better every day.
Take-over bids and GNP belt out the chorus:
it's not enough that sales graphs zoom
that inflation, so they say, is being deflated;
that's the smaller evil, only half the story,
it doesn't really matter, it's not enough
that arbitrators haunt the lonely corridors of hotels
lifting up their voices to declaim:

Things are getting better,
feel free, keep your cool, hang loose,
things are getting better   topsy turvy.
Here the United Church decides who's going to be boss
here the government washes Carter with white paper
and the rule is: be nice and nasty to each other

And that's the smaller evil
and I don't find it surprising
parliament debates in circles
and one side's just the same as the other
honest to God, scout's honour, here's where we live.

Here let them build their branch-plants
in this unowned no man's land
where soldiers shell out treats for Hallowe'en
and kidnappers hide like casual razor blades in apples.
Our cake is being sliced as we have baked it
in bits and pieces, no refunds, satisfaction guaranteed.

Here's where we stand on guard
and the consumer's waistline grows
and that's the smaller evil
and he veils his lost virility
with plastic party dolls
and acidly from his smoky den he calls:
yes, we want them to build their branch-plants.

In this kidnappers' cell
executive calendars flip the days past by themselves
while our past festers like inadequate sewage
and the future flashes ill-fitting dentures
and all because things are getting better

we're fixing things with inexpensive plastic
that's the way we do it, I don't find it surprising.

Snug as new notes in the mint we rest
where the just society's measured by Dow Jones
where stores that bulge with stock
lie fossilling in back of guarded glass.

The Centre for the Arts greets *Le Bourgeois Gentilhomme*
      with laughs in English
there's Can-Council exhibitions, stolen dynamite, Canadiana
      sales
and that's not all, only half the story
in this the untrue north, both weak and bound
this prosperous insanity that marches uniformed
in depleted sealskin coats, in limping time
through this century belonging to our innocence.

This country we thought different now's the same as others
and I feel guilty, and this guilt of mine's
the smaller evil, for here's the truth
which dupes, quite ordinary men, now dead,
broadcast from their graves but we don't hear
for we've laid concrete over all the earth.
Perhaps small screeches reach us in the dark
the bits and pieces gather till it forms a slab
gigantic tombstone

covering traces of old Vikings, voyageurs,
birches and canoes, the dinosaurs and polar bears,
the Donnellys, Laura Secord, those no longer here
the fish have choked on mercury
the cities stoned are climbing on the slab

and like those others, brief shuttling commuters,
how guilty I am made to feel; landlords holier-than-thou,
the natural gasmen, how they march together
with their leases, pipelines, how they stamp
in surrogate boots over thickening concrete
government-authorized haloes slack-noosed around their
      necks.

OK if these were people like all others
if it were still an ordinary country
and not this disappearing land, bogged down
with people whose innocence they cannot see is slipping
who don't know, don't want to know themselves
who have come to live inside this country
thinking they have fled but only from a similar country
who will be fleeing till they end beneath the slab.

If it were different it would be so much better
there'd be spring and sunshine
not this weedy and suspicious muddy land.

What am I doing here, why do I try
to unravel this unholy mess
of mailbox bombs and hangovers from expo,
prime minister's mini'd boosters, investment brokers
and find nothing but monolithic silence, four hundred
families and academic experts in control of people
barracked in apartments while soldiers stroll the streets.

This country, discontent and hungry,
meticulously splits itself apart,
suicide by proxy, heart dividing,
ticking like a fleshy bomb, opening like a wound.

Canada, 'tis of thee. . .
getting coverage now, more every day,
known to ordinary people elsewhere
these two nations separating
and here I am, prepared to mourn your separation
but asking, what's to be done

What's to be done is that which flickers at the tongue-tip
something as different as you are now but fused
that unafraid extends itself as one world
where concrete does not harden in the mouth.

Silenced with division, aghast and stifled,
breathless with our new predicament,
the *Globe and Mail, Le Devoir* breathless
(and that's the smaller evil)
this deafening lament that cannot recognize itself.
My just society, I want to keep my ignorance of you,
this kidnappers' cell into which I have been hurled
half living still, half alive,
that's where I am right now
I'm complaining but I'm not shifting
that's where I'll be for some time yet
till I move on to join the others
and stay, in a country then quite ordinary
we'll find elsewhere
not here.

Friday Afternoon at the Iowa City Airport

Dave Godfrey

Dave Godfrey is thirty-two years old and is married with three children. He is a Professor of English at Trinity College, University of Toronto, has written short stories for numerous anthologies, and is author and/or co-editor of *Death Goes Better with Coca-Cola, Man Deserves Man* (with Bill McWhinney), *Gordon to Watkins to You* (with Mel Watkins), and *The New Ancestors*.

Friday afternoon at the Iowa City Airport

DAVE GODFREY

If our tribe is degenerating and the former splendour of the kingdom vanishing – whence does it come, if not from the wrath of the tutelar spirits and the anger of the ances-tors! The thunder of the big guns has chased them, the noise of the Church bells does not please them, if they want to come to our help they are caught in the wires of the telephone. No wonder, therefore, if there are more and more evil men and if the power of our magic charms loses its potency. GHANAIAN CHIEF, 1900

No one can come to terms with violence rationally. Proof? Proof is the rational man's whore, says one violent voice within myself. Look, I am still willing to confess (confession is a means of coming to terms with violence), I was in the back seat of that battered Chrysler that delivered up Cross. I accept exile; it is a chosen humiliation. I hate the Black Panthers. I feel cheated that my death will not match that of Jens Munk: there death matched the life. If we had taken an American, he would not have lived sixty days.

Do you want to know more.

Fuck off.

It is morning. Light careens into the freight car and kicks some of the pain in my head. Without the voice I would never have been aware that some of the movement was exterior, however. C'est un abîme là. *Those are the words which saved my life for all this, for all this repetition. I was nineteen and playing the game of strikemaker. Yes, I was seeking violence. And seeing the open door I was about to jump out to renew the fight, now that I knew where I was. Yet now, now that I truly know where I am, I consider my state of innocence at that moment as the greatest gift my ancestors could have given. We cannot return to such givings easily. For, childhood fights aside, games aside, fantasy aside, violence had never really lived with me, had lived with me but never shattered limb nor path. Instead I sought it out. Out of nothing but innocence can one search for violence.* C'est un abîme là: *young Jean Pitou stated the fact. Korpella we hated, and Korpella, mill-owner and lumberman, hated us in similar form. Korpella's thugs were brothers and cousins of the bush foreman and they had laid us carefully into that freight-car heading empty for the prairies. Unconscious. With the door unlocked. If we had wanted to leap, or roll, out of that moving safety down a cliff of rock to lie dead in an unknown lake, that remained our choice. They too preferred battles.* C'est un abîme là, 'tenntion: *Jean said out of his own head-ringing pain.*

I like to think the cosh was made of ironwood.

Man has three fantasies: sex, slaughter and utopia. And I like to think they come to his life in that order, at least in terms of arriving with sufficient force to function as determiners of action.

I am not only trying to be precise: I am trying to confuse you because I am confused myself. You see, when I was young, the Americans stole my first sex fantasy from me, and I have always hated them for that. Which is why I am glad it was Langlois, the bush foreman's boxer son who slugged me from behind with whatever length of pipe, or clenched fist, or, hopefully, ironwood he had chosen. So it was him I hated violently first. Jean always said it felt like pipe. I can ignore the fact that the union headquarters were in Minneapolis. After all, we had sought them out. And it was a CN diesel hauling Jean and me into that cold awakening. But what greasy path did Marilyn (naked, with blond curls covering nothing of those two perfect breasts of lust) follow to steal the doorway of sexual fantasy from that younger me.

I dream of Super Fortresses dropping reams and reams of photographic Asian beauties upon the farms and ghettos of America, you see; revenge is our common monster.

The only *fact* of which I am certain is that I enjoyed the shame which was potentially there, beside me, within that battered Chrysler for suddenly the counter-symbolism was there: *they* had the power but *they* were escorting *us* to a kind of freedom. They were afraid. And there was no dynamite. Shit. We didn't really have time, you know. I shall not mention the religious medal. Have you not thought of that already, yourself? Does the chain tighten about your neck or is that your hand which burns with the twisting? Be honest. Forget the firing squad you have planned for us in Civic Square. Do you not now accept at least that the Brinks trucks constituted a violence?

Once I knifed a girl.

No child dreams of heaven. I am not sure if the arousal of Utopia has yet caroused in my brain. Perhaps it was that childhood protein deficiency. Utopia has no organ: what do you expect from a few hundred generations? There is no climax to ease its incipient itchings. No Marilyn-succubus hiding somewhere there among the sperm and shaving-cream. No feeling of glory as the raven-black oil from the Gulf pipeline spills back to the Saskatchewan earth at last – after the rifle shot from the stolen Piper Aztec. Please note that I am not thinking simply of that authority-beauty which comes when you know your children trust in you. I am thinking of that impossible utopia, that impossible trust between families, between tribes. Do you have an organ for that?

Thus I study witches a good deal, in an historic fashion. That seems to me more important than study of the imposition of the War Measures Act. You know of course, historical technicians, that my grandfather imposed the War Measures Act himself. On the way to France. With a flick of his officer's baton. As he walked out of his Saskatchewan homestead towards the muddy playing fields of the one great home. So I know how that was done. But there is nothing of witches in the direct family history.

And there are lessons to be learned from the use of witchcraft in the extermination of the Knight Templars. You see we become what we fight. The choice is here Indians or Americans. The FLQ are Indians or Americans. It did not take the Christians many hours in power before they adopted the methods of those who had sought to exterminate them. *You see we become what we fight.* Robert Weaver knows this: which is why he has chosen to be a good Indian and write editorials about Leacock's birthday. And I am going to die an American, defending my son's right to choose to become a peaceful Indian. Yes, this is indeed all metaphors. Love is an end to love.

We become quickly what we fight. It is another afternoon. Late in spring. I am about to fly from Iowa City, Iowa to a secluded fishing camp on the Restigouche. And I am wacking-off hatred. Its sweet lust pervades my being. I have a simple plan to stop the police action in Viet Nam. It is the spring of 1966. A long, long time ago. Longer ago somehow than when my barely-haired balls first plunged into Marilyn's photographic mysteries. So much visible hatred and humiliation bounces off the assurance of the three crew-cut soldiers who are busy saying farewell to their crew-cutted fathers that it becomes impossible for me not to hate them – no – this is so many lies. It is easy for me to hate them. Easy. Easy. As easy as it is to take over the plane. Now I can't even remember how I killed them. But they were all dead when the DC-3 plunged into that lake far north of Superior. I knew it was deep because I had almost plunged into it myself once. Some instinct took me there. I swam up to the railway embarkment and crawled slowly up the stones towards the steel rails. It took me two days to walk back to civilization.

But that didn't stop the war after all, did it? Perhaps if I had found the nerve to continue? But perhaps it did put off My Lai for as much as a year. Think of that possibility, my liberal technicians. Was there something in Lieutenant Calley's mind which paralleled mine, which *knew* that he was preventing some more awful slaughter. Are you going to confess your own violence-masturbations after this, my friends. That is my only purpose. I don't really pretend that you are interested in my theory of witches.

I joined the FLQ in 1966, although I had intellectually considered such choice since at least 1964. Prior to that I was an American. But then there was that knifed girl. You may not know the Restigouche river. It forms the boundary between Quebec and New Brunswick and it is a song.

Two species of animals live in that song. I thought I deserved to be one of the rich animals. Deserving of fishing for the melodic salmon, the Restigouche salmon, voices of mystics and sages: I will not sully their flights with words within this foulness. But you know what I am saying, eh? The President of a Drug Corporation, the President of Colt Industries, old Monet, the husband of a banking heiress, Mr. Burton, Mr. Weldon, Mr. Phipps. You know what I am confessing, eh, and you want me to get on with it?

We stood around one pool in which the perfect greeness of body of those magical salmon shone like some message from Leviathan. And we did not fish. Two Scottish guides and I. Christ, why do we not have a clean, common name for ourselves? Our selves who gleamed downward into that American-possessed pool, eager to snare the magic, but held back, held back by what generations of negation. My ancestors were bond servants in Rhode Island: I have no common name for ourselves and the battered, hungry ones who circled in rust-rotted Chryslers on the hills high above that pool. I want them all clean and eager and full and proud and my brothers in this land of the mystic and silvery salmon. That is why I hate America – because I did not fish in that pool which the nineteen Americans and two Canadians had leased for fifty thousand dollars. You know the clubhouse, eh? You know how easy it would be to place the dynamite beneath the flagpole. You know whose flag flies there alone. You have thought of the peace that would be between you and your brothers who would come down from the circling hills in their bush jackets and black, tight-ankle pants.

And one of them would be Langlois and sandbag me back to the lake which holds the DC-3. Eh? I haven't yet come to the dullness of witches and Trudeau and already you have deserted me for facts and theories. It would be better if you began your own confession. Damn it, if some of you don't soon I shall start another organization which will scare the shit out of you. It will be called the RCMP and it will have the power to arrest everyone who does not confess his love of terror.

Do you believe in telenomy? In Quarton's cognitive dissonance? Is that what you see in Quebec? In me? System instabilities: anxiety, anger, over-assertion, over-aggression; withdrawal, melancholy, nausea. Do you really believe with Platt that the sudden, swift, unforseen, simplifying pattern is right around the corner? Do you believe in hierarchical growth? (i–1–i+1) appeals to you then? You accept that IBM is a properly functioning subsystem about which to build the great leap to a new society?

Myself, when I drive off the Parkway and see that massive, red, brain-fortress, with its mitre of a private exit from Eglinton, I think constantly of dynamite. Fuck off, Charlie, of course I'm some kind of a fanatic nut. Gross brain disfunction. Symbolic disorder in my medial amygdala. If you're so fucking smart, why don't you know what the amygdala is? Soon your technicians will be operating on mine. I have already felt the electrodes. The attack pattern is characteristic of the species even when artificially stimulated.

But no worry. I won't make the one mistake. This confession is a lucky break for you. Luckily my cell has already infiltrated the RCMP. My last mistake was the blond girl from Minneapolis. At Holy Child School in Ghana. We had just started to play and the equipment was faulty from the constant sweat of the sun. And we were playing polluted shit: Ray Charles and Beatles and just a little of the real Glen Warren. Christ, we had sold her all but the jacks of our souls, why did she have to tell us that the nuns wanted to hear the latest hits by the Great Global Village, fresh from Minneapolis? The fucking stupidity of it impressed even the judges and my sentence was short.

This is your perversion, Pierre Trudeau. To use that vision of order and peace within which this nation was founded (and yes, yes, my Brownell grandfathers predicted all of this, in detail, when they left Rhode Island for the rocks of Nova Scotia) in order to continue that visionless, piecemeal tattered, treacherous, gut-hungry vending of our joint sovereignty to the madmen of the south.

Are you simply asking that we rise up to strike you? Is that your current violence-masturbation? Do you take on the FLQ and the FLC at once. I heard you in Nova Scotia stating your counter vision. I saw your police seize Scanlon's on orders from the White House. I know what your witchhunters will do when you find me. Shall I interpret all those facts for you? We are to be allowed to produce spare Barbie Dolls for our good neighbours who intend to immerse themselves almost completely in service industries, eh? Fuck that. Your vision is matched by that of the good doctor who took a flask of Crown Royal to revive "our boys" in the POW camps. I do not wish to pass that on to my son. End of confession. Underground again. Opening of hostilities.

Violence Language and the Body Politic

John O'Neill

John O'Neill is Professor and Chairman of the Department of Sociology at York University. He is the author, editor and translator of a number of articles and books on the philosophical problems of Marxism. His more recent work is in social phenomenology and ethnomethodology from which there will be forthcoming *Making Sense Together* and *Sociology and the Body-Politic.*

Violence, language and the body politic

JOHN O'NEILL

> *No doubt we are sensible in giving names to places: Canada, the Argentine. But we would also be sensible to remember that the land we have given these names to, and all but the relatively very small human population, wear these names lightly.* JAMES AGEE

There are times indeed when Canada wears her name lightly, a symbol of peace for the world, a land of forests and lakes still new to her people. But nowadays the name of Canada sinks in the land twisted by terrorism and fearful for the unity of its people.

The experience of violence tests in us the sense of our own humanity. It may provoke in us the cry of our own anger, rage and sorrow felt for the very first time. In some it will lead to despair and silence. Terror commits its deepest injury when it tempts us to silence. Yet it is not easy to say what we feel in the face of terror for at such times to speak at all is to depend upon the very human motives and situations which terror destroys. Thus terror hollows and empties our language, threatening it with destruction and ultimate silence.

How, then, are we to speak of terror and violence which obliterate the human landscape and wither the look of man? We need to dwell among men to begin to understand how it is we find violence among our other experiences like love or disappointment, joy and anger. We know about violence just as we know about famine and floods, or the coming of the jumbo jet and thalidomide babies. We know that there is violence in the streets in which white and blacks and police and students are involved in our own towns, in Berkeley, Tokyo, Paris and London, even Toronto. What child does not know of Vietnam? What parent does not know of Hiroshima, Auschwitz and Biafra? Our common awareness of violence easily draws distinctions within the forms and modes of violence as it affects our daily practices. We distinguish war and revolutions, political violence and criminal violence. We also distinguish personal violence and institutional violence, the blow on the head and the hunger and disease which results from foreign exploitation. We know of these things from life in the family, from the hurts of love and in general, from the very business of living that ties the world together in a patchwork of wealth and misery. We know of racial violence, urban and colonial violence and what we know in general of these is not much less than the experts whom these phenomena produce.

We have then, through everyday language a capacity for living with violence. Even Hiroshima was not experienced in the same way by everyone and so there were some left to help, and to pray and to rebuild. Indeed, the phenomenon of violence is curiously revealing of the nature of human space and human time, that is to say, of the human world as the frame and flesh of violence and imagination. Every day we turn away a poor man. Every day we ride through ghettos on overhead expressways, in automobiles for which the exploitation of the world's natural resources is the primary symbol of affluent pride and colonial indignity. Every evening we watch living death and destruction on news reels just as all day long, day in and day out, we and our children, but especially our children, watch hours of violent action as the medium of a primitive sense of right and wrong, the code of criminal justice. And yet we celebrate, as we must, the great tissue of human understanding woven out of our common need of each other's love and labour. We need to believe that the contiguity of space is human, that our neighbour fares no worse than ourselves.

Violence is not simply any threat to the stability of the political and social order. For in everyday politics, change and reform are as much sought after as stability and entrenchment. Under ordinary circumstances we do not speak of violence to convey the expectation of the legitimate enforcement of political mandates. We understand the power of government and we trust that it will carry out its will with due regard for humanity and with provisions for appeal. Nor are these conventional understandings in any way naive. They are the very fabric of political order. For this reason they are provided for in the institutions of law, parliamentary practice, democratic election and the freedom of speech and publicity. The conviction that government is not naked force, that justice is not terror, and that democracy is not merely a sham elitism is not to be regarded as a mere article of political faith unless it can be shown that none of the institutions of political life served its purpose and that there is no public domain in which this faith can be acted upon through political deeds and public speech to which man attend.

The concern with violence is mere sensationalism when it is not understood in terms of an analysis of the fabric of the social order which generates violence and its onlookers. For we should not overlook that we are the consumers of violence as much as its producers, though not in the same way and with the result that there is a certain order in the variety of concerns with violence. Violence is tragic when it is not willed yet unavoidable. In every other case it is comic, mad and utterly senseless feeding upon its own frustration. Historically, violence has ranged anywhere from political slapstick to the cold war games of mega-destruction. But the experience of our century is with a scale of violence that overwhelms social science knowledge and reduces it to fictional extrapolations of the origins and consequences of violence in utopian orders beyond genuine political experience.

The tendency of social science knowledge to produce fictional states or utopias in order to make sense of its own production arises from the failure to comprehend the political context of knowledge, speech and action. This is the task of political phenomenology and it is in this sense that we might turn to Hannah Arendt's essay *On Violence* for what it can teach us about the foundations of political life which so much concern us in Canada. This is an exercise which will, I think, reward our concern to create a political culture able to domesticate the massive forces of modern technology and to comprehend the symbiosis of modern rationality and violence.

It would be easy to dismiss Miss Arendt's essay as a conventional attempt at orientation in an academic world which for its own violence now looks more like the world beyond its walls. For at first sight, Miss Arendt seems to pose the threat of world destruction as a mere pretext for the discussion of student rebellions and the violence of Marxist rationalism. Yet it is clearly impossible for her to have anything very revealing to say about the empirical contexts and developments on topics of such range in the short compass she allows herself. But we must remember that Miss Arendt has already written at length in *The Human Condition* of political foundations and modern world destruction as a problem in the very nature of modern knowledge.

With this in mind, I propose to read Miss Arendt's essay *On Violence* as a phenomenology of the basic vocabulary of politics, motivated by the tendency of violence to destroy the foundations of political speech and to undermine the realm of politics. And I propose this reading conscious that it is not to be found there entirely except as a further exercise in political imagination, hopefully within the spirit of her own reflections and without conceit.

The modern age is built upon the paradox that its expansion of technological, economic and social activity has produced a massive world alienation, an attitude of world-domination and universal migration motivated by what Weber called "innerworldly asceticism." The release of these forces was preceded by the collapse of the ancient and feudal conceptions of the world as a political realm of public deeds and public speech resting upon the citizen's or the lord's control of his own household and its private economy. So long as the household economy was embedded in the political order, men's labour served to produce objects whose value was subordinate to the social values created by the thoughts, deeds and speech of political man. The modern world, however, is built upon an inordinate expansion of individual utilities which subordinates labour or production to a cycle of consumption and destruction disembedded from the political order. This is the source of the modern conception of "society" as a field solely of individual interests which inspired Hobbes' nasty vision and whose essentially contradictory features were later explored by Hegel and Marx.

Marcuse has argued that affluent slavery is fun mediated by the techniques of repressive desublimation – the executive pink shirt, and that ambiguously available "Mary" from the Royal Bank. This is an argument which is tempting to Miss Arendt inasmuch as the resulting smoothness of progress and the inevitable widening of the gap between contrived and human needs invites violence as the only possible means of interrupting a course of events that threatens to automate dehumanization. Although this is only a remark she makes in passing, it must be pointed out that it serves more to identify the violence of affluent student youth or American despair than the violence of workers' strikes or of the ghetto and colonial poor.

Miss Arendt has herself pointed to the pain of bodily labour as the essence of modern experience affecting the masses. Her account in fact resembles Marx's description of the alienation of the worker not just from his product, but from his other sensory and intersubjective possibilities. Labour's desire to break with the privatization of experience through bodily pain is surely the most basic cause of the revolutionary violence which Miss Arendt considers essential to the cause of humanity. The problem is that the pain of labour and its daily and world routine of misery, hidden in the mines, ships and factories, finds no expression, not even by the workers themselves. For we should not be deceived into believing that Marxism, or the languages of conventional politics and social science speak in the voice of the workers. Here the workers are not to be seen or heard. For this reason their very appearance surprises us and is a threat to the political order which nearly always responds to them with violence. Moreover the frustrations of labour are aggravated in an affluent culture where the over-privatization of social resources worked by monopoly capitalism results in a stylization of the issues of power, class and public indifference. The result is a fun-culture riddled with violence, racism and colonial wars. The basic class conflict underlying the social order of monopoly capitalism is further distorted through the techniques of repressive desublimation into the sentimentalities of charity, social reform and colonial aid which are the vicarious counterparts of affluent fun-culture and its white liberal politics. In such a context, it becomes very difficult to speak of justice and outrage which calls for unavoidable violence because these are responses that have been made "irrational" through the passive "rationalization" of motives worked upon the card carrying members of the fun-culture whose political future has been mortgaged by this same process. It belongs to this same context that violence is made to appear "senseless," just as the exploitation which causes it, for want of any adequate sociological analysis, is considered "unnecessary". This is so in part because cynics consider the class system can be sustained without overt exploitation, and for the rest because the "solution" of the production problem reduces exploitation to a problem of improved patterns of social consumption.

Violence however, can also be made part of the 'realism' of capitalist fun-culture. By this I mean that the split between domestic peace and international violence can be reproduced as the split in the animal and rational nature of man. The colonies, ghettos and now the prehistory of man provide marvellous scenarios for the dramatization of the destructive potential of a superficially harmless fun-culture.

Since Miss Arendt has not, in my opinion, been sufficiently sympathetic to colonial and racial violence or its romantic interpreters, something more may be said of it as an expression of the pain of labour outside of the fun-culture.

Fanon and Cleaver have shown how well the rhetoric of mind-body dualism is suited to the expression of racial exploitation and colonial revolt and thus how the language of violence is essential to the body politic.

Eldridge Cleaver, black soul on ice, understands instinctively the contemporary reversal of the ideal and material orders in North American civilization. Since Cassius Clay affected poetry, the Word is no longer white property to teach blacks the lesson of submission, the great white dualism of class and the mind-body split. Worse still for American white male supremacy, it was a black muscle-man who betrayed their fears, Muhammad Ali spouting poetry, floating like a butterfly, stinging like a bee. But Cleaver himself undertands deepest of all the demon of Black poetry, the blinding White Circle of the Black soul.

> A cult of death need of the simple striking arm under the street lamp. The cutters from under their rented earth. Come up, black dada nihilismus. Rape the white girls. Rape their fathers. Cut the mothers' throats.

In his allegory of the Black Eunuchs, Cleaver looks into the face of his own anger and what he sees there should give us pause lest we speak too easily of reform or revolution. He sees the hatred between whites and blacks so twisted into the roots of the black family that there can be no love that isn't broken by the black's lust for a white woman or the black woman's secret admiration for the white man unbroken by the system. In a racist context the class struggle roots itself in the individual's split-self, dividing the black male and female against themselves and destroying the natural unit of a black society, a black nation or homeland. Thus the black man suffers a socially imposed self-hatred of his manhood compounded by the stereotypification of the black as brute strength, body without mind. In terms of this analysis the black revolution can only succeed if it involves a deep psychic transformation, the rebirth of black pride, of the black spirit, of the black family and black culture. This is not to deny the place of violence in the black revolution. But I think Cleaver means to say that there is much potential violence that is the violence of twisted souls who must also pass through their own dark night before the blood flows in the streets and before anyone can be sure his is building the new Africa.

The same profound diagnosis of the black experience is developed in Frantz Fanon's essays on colonial social structure and the psychology of slavery and revolt. Fanon makes it clear that the way oppression works is through the black man's dreams, through his sexual and family life and through taste. of self-hatred and oppression. Here too the medium is his language which teaches him the contours, the touch and the message. Language, knowledge, beauty, power, money, the land are all WHITE and the black man who uses or looks upon any of these instinctively warns himself off, as a thief, a violator, a brute negativity. To be in the world at all is for the black man to leave his home and his woman and even his senses for the white man's world. This a daily routine, a journey of the soul made everytime the black man leaves the ghetto for work in the morning, passing a policeman, a home or any white man whose look tells him there is another way but it is not for blacks. Fanon has the marvellous gift of revealing the structure of racial neurosis as a landscape, a country, a language, a dream, a vision of the body in which black and white confront each other as themselves. In the white man's neurosis the black man figures as the force of life that is drying up on himself. In his own dream the black man dreams of white civilization.

Miss Arendt remarks on the irony of interpreting the violence generated by the world's most complex industrial technology as due to man's basically animal need for violence which, if frustrated by culture, then takes such "irrational" forms as world destruction rather than the more natural periodic displays of war and violence. It is in her reply to the attempt to place the definition of the uses of violence in the hands of the new political zoologists such as Lorenz, Ardrey, Rubin and Hoffman that Miss Arendt's conception of *the essentially human nature of violence* is set forth.

The tendency of technological rationality to generate social and political values is the basic feature of modern politics. At the same time, it is the source of the wars, revolutions and violence that constitute the contemporary crisis of political authority. We should not fail to understand her argument on the human or humanizing nature of violence. The attempt to reduce violence to an irrational factor, to deprive it of any place in the vocabulary of politics, can only be successful where the processes of dehumanization have reduced men to abject slavery and victimage. It is only where men see no prospect of action that their sense of injustice and rage at alterable human conditions atrophies or is turned against themselves. In short, violence and rage must be understood as integral motives so long as the institutions of political conduct are open to human initiative and the call for freedom and justice. Miss Arendt warns against the tendency to place the human emotions in opposition to "rationality" when in fact these emotions only become "irrational" when they sense reason itself is distorted. Indeed, so much of what outrages contemporary rationality is nothing but the outrage of a more humane reasonableness driven to expose the sham of establishment rationality. It is in this context that we must understand the rhetoric of creative violence, that is to say, as the attempt to connect with the humane roots of reason which are progressively destroyed by technological rationality and the myth of progress.

Miss Arendt is critical of the attempt to reduce violence to a biological concept which is then reintroduced as a dangerous metaphor in the vocabulary of revolutionary politics. Here I think she is not always in touch with the language of revolution which belongs to a general cultural revolution and is first of all the work of poets and artists who restore language and perception to playfulness, to say what is unspeakable, to make the word flesh once more. In this, the language of revolution reaches naturally for the language of the body because its experience is the awareness of the body starved, brutalized and ready to kill or be killed.

The eroticism of modern economic and political life is the fundamental feature of the major events or happenings which move the body politic. The counterparts of the happy, healthy, integrated executive and his suburban family are the long-haired visionaries of flowers and rainbows who are the soul-brothers of sit-ins, lunch-ins, ride-ins and love-ins which are the renewal of the libidinal body politic. The phenomena of violence in the ghettos, mass demonstrations and sit-ins in the offices of authority are all grounded in the basic logic of the body politic: not to endure the unendurable, not to suffer inhuman denials of recognition and in ultimate crises to "come together" so that the authorities can "see" what they are doing to the people. The underlying logic is a logic of demonstration that is pre-ideological and rests upon the simple faith that men have in the renewal of justice and community It is a simple logic which challenges the constitutional alienation of the authority of the body politic. For once the injustice of life in the ghetto goes beyond the limits of tolerance, then the ghetto becomes a natural armoury of stones, bottles, sticks, crowds, with which to beat the conventional police-system. Once the inanity of administrative authority is exposed it is defenseless against the belly-laugh, the clap-in or sing-in. Where is the official who will explain to children and to young men and women with flowers the necessity of the war that will cripple them or blow them to bits?

It may be that we are engaged in a new meta-politics in which the Burkean identification of temporality and political community is destroyed in the politics of the generation gap and the street happenings of the "new mutuants." The new style of political demonstration destroys the polis as an organization of need and wants, of life and against death, by pushing death into the erotic economy of male-female, black-white, rich-poor, expert-layman organization. The politics of unisex, nudity, camp and pop art exhibit the reversibility of organization, artist and audience, leader and mass whose own self-improvization and abandonment is the supreme anti-political act. Leslie Fiedler has spoken of the flight from *polis* to *thiasos* ("the movement"). This involves a new direction of political knowledge which surpasses the Victorian misgivings of Lionel Tiger's genetic code of male-bonding no less than Fiedler's own anxiety over the post-Jewish antics of the anti-male. The new politics is Dionysian, achieving form only in the moment of self-destruction. Because it maintains control through improvization, the new politics cannot presume upon any rationalization or ideological interpretation of sensory experience. Its audience is therefore part of the art, the music, the lesson and the political platform. The new politics invents a destruction of vicarious experience in becoming children, playing with toys, dressing up, mocking, loving and raging in the streets. Its destruction of vicarious experience is simultaneously the creation of community groups, circles and games in which experience is opened to feeling, magic and mysticism in the search for a workable and communicable truth. The way of this truth is often stark and violent. It differs from the established truth in its search to become a truth, founded upon the gift and the exigency of the human body.

These observations, however, imply no endorsement whatsoever of the use of biological metaphors which propose violence as the cure for a sick society, sick with white guilt and black rage. Violence may serve as a means to the dramatization of the political condition. The risk in resorting to violence is that it proposes itself as a solution to racial and ethnic differences caught in the deadlock of interests which liberal society refuses to give a genuine political definition.

So long as these interests lack the vocabulary of class politics their actions can be reduced to crimes against property or decency as purely criminal or police concerns. This anti-political character of violence regarded from the standpoint of law and order in turn feeds back into such violence driving it into terrorism in ever more desperate attempts to expose the political and social segregation of the issues of poverty, race and war. This cycle is only aggravated where the establishment power is organized in bureaucracies which increasingly privatize the contexts of meaning and action at the expense of the political realm. The result is a certain pathological symbiosis between bureaucratic rationality and the resort to vocabularies of creative violence, internal migration and communal utopias which destroy genuine political speech and public action.

Bureaucracy destroys the political realm because it treats individuality as equality and thereby destroys its sense as uniqueness which brings into being the necessity for human

94

speech and expression. Bureaucracy stylizes differences as fads or fashions creating the political paradox of conformist freedoms. Corporate capitalism in particular parodies human initiative through the engineering of responses to the inevitability of annual novelties. It drowns the question of who a man is in the litanies of what he has or can acquire in order to construct an image. These effects of bureaucracy are perfectly geared to the liberal minimization of the public realm of common action once inspired by collective identity and tradition in which character and history interweave. The modern world systematically destroys the special and temporal dimensions of public conduct through the privatization of the resources of action and its codes of meaning and motivation.

richmond   Jean Marchand

In North America, religion, politics and business are alike in being serious business. There is no joy in them, and thus their very seriousness is inverted into the vulgarities of worship, democracy and money-making. We must, however, understand that profanity or vulgarity can only be what it is in the light of its fall from the sacred. Politics, religion and business are equally holy works of man. It is the task of the rebel, the clown and the practical joker to remind us of the dialects of the holy and the profane, of godhead and manhood.

The vocation of western knowledge for domination establishes modern science as the paradigm of social and political knowledge. Its behavioural assumptions invent plausible utopias of colossal world violence and destruction while alienating the human responses of outrage and violence as appeals against their injustice and insanity.

Modern violence is of such an enormous scope and impersonality that it strains every metaphor of language by which we might tie events to their authors and victims. There is the massive horror but there is no one to speak about; only the author's guilt in his own survival which reduces his language to the barest medium of factual account and reporting. And this is perhaps necessary in order to save language from delirium in the effort to speak at all of modern violence, to be faithful at once to what happened and to the necessity of rediscovering the human face, the minds and hearts of those buried or crippled by these experiences. The scene of violence, the camp, the bomb, the riot, overwhelm the categories of character, intentionality and action so that not even the writer can situate himself, far less construct a conventional story. Modern armies obliterate a village or town before they can enter it and when they do, the villages are empty or littered with dead and maimed bodies with no other story to tell than the ravages of overkill and napalm whose meaning is reduced to the scene itself.

Language is the soul of our lives together. Today we must work to restore language, to speak where violence puts an end to speech. Miss Arendt's essay *On Violence* begins the work of renewing political speech, defining its basic words and the contexts of public and private usage which generate their meaning. In this task the only resources we have are the same words which condemn a man to death, or prejudice and exploitation. There are times when words take refuge in songs, jokes and prayers. But the soul of language is never broken while men still have on their lips, the words of "freedom", "justice", "faith" and "revolution".

* * *

We are bound by local facts and there is a kind of goodness in this. It makes what we know belong to our place and time like the other things men produce in the great variety of their labours. The provinces of Canada are regions of poetry but also of misery and exploitation and of the sadness of our land. Today our troubles are immediate, our sorrows personal. Yet we need to reflect upon them as universal concerns. And so our first sorrows must find the language of all sorrow.

Rebuilding a
Free Society

Alan Borovoy

Mr. Borovoy was educated at the University of Toronto (B.A. B.LL). He was admitted to the Bar of Ontario at Osgoode Hall in 1959. In 1961 he organized a successful lobby for Ontario legislation against racial discrimination, and in 1962 he assisted in the organization of human rights activities in Halifax, involving in particular the problems of the Negro slum, Africville. In 1965 he was the chief white organizer of the march by 450 Indians in Kenora, Ontario, which resulted in government compliance with every demand of the Indian brief. His writings include articles for *Canadian Labour, Saturday Night*, and the Toronto Globe & Mail. Mr. Borovoy is presently the General Counsel of the Canadian Civil Liberties Association.

Rebuilding a free society

A. ALAN BOROVOY

The wholesale suspension of civil liberties represents our first response to entry upon the age of violence. Soon we shall have to pick up the pieces and make some hard decisions. Once we recognize that our pre-October tranquility is not recoverable within the foreseeable future, how shall we respond? What adjustments are necessary in a society where urban terror may be part of normal life? Shall we answer subsequent provocations with a suspension of civil liberties? Shall we legislate additional police powers and greater restrictions on a more permanent basis? In short, how will Canada cope with the loss of her innocence?

This article will not deal with the propriety of the Government's decision to adopt emergency powers. In other contexts, I have answered this in the negative. Nor will this article deal with the propriety of the Government's *ever* adopting emergency powers. In other contexts, I have answered this in the affirmative.

These issues have already been debated at great length. What we have only begun to address, however, is what will remain after the revocation of these powers. To what extent will we and should we suffer *permanent* invasions of our traditional freedoms? This is now a more vital consideration.

The comments from official quarters seem to be indicating the direction that we might take. The Prime Minister of Canada has warned us about the possibility of police surveillance on the campuses. The Quebec Minister of Justice has made a number of suggestions about the need for compulsory identity cards and even press censorship. The lack of controversy which has greeted these pronouncements reveals a growing willingness on the part of the Canadian public to sustain a more permanent diminution of our traditional freedoms.

On the other hand, the long-term battle against political terrorism may require not a curtailment but an *enlargement* of our fundamental freedoms. The more we reduce the avenues and the protections for non-violent dissent, the more we incur the risk that dissent will become violent. In an era of deeply felt social grievances between ethnic groups, income groups, and age groups there will be inevitable pressure for substantial change. If the groups seeking change do not feel that the law affords them a fair opportunity to advance their cause through non-violent means, greater numbers of them will resort to or at least endorse violent means. The greatest danger is that otherwise, responsible citizens will either sympathize with or decline to oppose political violence. Thus, while our society is legitimately concerned with providing short term protections against the threat of violent dissent, it must simultaneously provide long term avenues for the expression of non-violent dissent.

In a few months, the emergency powers will be revoked. The problem is how to adjust our short and long term strategies during the period of the new normalcy which will succeed revocation. To what extent will the impending challenges require a change in our legal safeguards?

Police Powers – A Short Term Response to Terror

What is the case for the post-crisis expansion of police powers? It is one thing to justify additional powers when there is a real state of apprehended insurrection. But when the *Public Order Act* is revoked, even the Government will be admitting then that there will be no imminent insurrectionist peril. Against what peril then will we need greater powers on a permanent basis? Against terror? Bombings? The possibility of future insurrections?

The onus is on those who would invade our liberties to demonstrate the size of the evil to be purged and the need for the means to be used. Fear is no substitute for thought; faith is no substitute for facts. Evidence of danger and analysis of need are the necessary conditions for a reduction in the freedoms of a free society.

Any proposals for expanded police power must take proper cognizance of their regular powers. Even a cursory examination will reveal that regular police powers are far from inconsiderable.

Essentially, police powers divide into two broad categories – secret information-gathering and open intrusions. The first category includes infiltration, intelligence, and surveillance. The second category includes searches, seizures, arrests, and detentions.

How extensive are the normal police powers of open intrusion? Under the Criminal Code a police officer may arrest without warrant anyone who he has reasonable and probable grounds to believe has committed or is about to commit an indictable offence. He may obtain a warrant to enter a place for search and seizure upon demonstrating to a judicial officer reasonable and probable grounds to believe that the premises in question contain evidence of a criminal offence. Where he reasonably believes that dangerous weapons offences are being committed, he may search without warrant persons and places other than dwelling houses. He may enter without warrant virtually any place including a dwelling house, which he has reasonable and probable grounds to believe is harbouring a person whom he is entitled to arrest. In the absence of dire emergency, it is difficult to conceive why the police would need powers of open intrusion beyond these rather substantial ones.

The powers of secret information-gathering are, at present, virtually unlimited. Almost nothing in law prevents the police from infiltrating, spying, bribing, and even engaging in electronic eavesdropping. While a valid case might be made that some of these powers should be curtailed, particularly wiretapping and electronic eavesdropping, it is impossible to argue for their expansion. What could be urged, of course, is the more skilful *use* of some of these techniques.

When considering the powers of the police, it would be also wise to bear in mind one of the most significant statements that emerged during the course of the crisis. At one stage, Quebec Premier Robart Bourassa warned his constituents that even the assumption of totalitarian powers could not assure the level of security which we desire. Indeed, there may be little short-term protection which is possible against a small hard core of violent fanatics. Paradoxically, while they are not large enough to possess an all-out insurrectionist capacity, they might be relatively invulnerable to the preventive powers of the state. Even though they cannot overthrow the Government, they can inflict substantial havoc through sporadic sniping, bombing, kidnapping, and assassination. All that is required is a small group of fanatics who are willing to die for their cause. Even the totalitarian powers of the Soviet Union, or as we are witnessing, of fascist Spain,

101

are not enough to prevent all the damage within the capability of a small number of committed terrorists.

The great danger arising from some of these terrorist groups is that the threshold of safety we desire may be, for some time, an unattainable illusion. But in the quest for it, we may, ourselves, erode the very freedoms we seek to protect. We might surrender a substantial amount of liberty without purchasing a desirable amount of security.

In any event, at this point the proponents of expanded permanent police powers have failed to make their case. They have demonstrated neither the magnitude of the perils we face nor the inadequacy of the powers we have. Apart from a clear and present danger of the illegal seizure of Government, why can't we rely on present police power to provide society with a realistic level of adequate protection? Indeed, why can't the skilful use of those powers prevent the emergence of a clear and present danger? Without satisfactory answers, we should brook no further encroachments.

The Right to Dissent – A Long Term Response to Terror

So much for our short term strategies. But what of the long term strategies? Is the right of and opportunity for non-violent dissent sufficiently guaranteed at present? Is the law fair enough to deprive the violent revolutionaries of sizeable constituencies? In my view, the law in these areas has been defective for a long time. It is potentially repressive and inadequately protective of legitimate non-violent dissent. Moreover, in the aftermath of emergency powers, the political climate may now be more conducive than ever to the actual use of the repressive instruments at our disposal. During the recent debates about the invocation of emergency powers, many claims were made that the existing law was adequate to cope with the perceptible threats to public order. In my opinion, the existing substantive law is not only adequate, but it is also excessive. The wisest preparation for the termination of emergency powers may lie in the liberalization of normal powers.

The Importance and the Limits of Free Speech

One of the most vital vehicles for the promotion of social

change is freedom of speech. The right of free speech enables us to mobilize the support of others in order to rectify the wrongs for which we seek redress. Unjust governments and unjust policies are not likely to survive in an atmosphere of free public debate. However, although vital and central, freedom of speech is not and cannot be an absolute. There are some circumstances where other values must prevail. One such value is the social peace. No society can countenance the exercise of speech which precipitates a substantial disruption of peace. As Oliver Wendell Holmes wisely counselled us, there can be no freedom of speech to shout "Fire" in a crowded theatre where there is no fire. In a situation of great physical disorder and violence, there is no meaningful enjoyment of anything, including freedom of speech.

Thus the real issue is how to create a sensible balance between the competing claims of free speech and public order. It is my view that the present law is out of balance. It leans too heavily and unnecessarily toward the protection of peace at the expense of speech. In a number of situations the law restricts the right to speak where the threat to the peace is non-existent, minimal, or capable of adequate protection in other ways. The post-crisis era will require, as never before, the quest for a proper balance. To whatever extent we encroach without need on the freedom of speech, we will promote in our midst the support of violence.

It will be helpful to explore some of the present legal provisions which contain restrictions against free speech. Where possible, we should indicate to what extent the restriction is unwarranted and in what direction reform might lie.

Sedition

The sedition offences purport to punish the person who "teaches or advocates . . . the use, without authority of law, of force as a means to accomplish a governmental change within Canada". Not only does the law prohibit an *act* of force aimed at accomplishing a governmental change, but it also prohibits *speech* in support of such force. What we legitimately seek to prevent are acts of violence. The issue is: at what point in the continuum between the thought and the deed is it appropriate for the law to intervene? Speech which is likely to result in violent deeds is sufficiently dangerous to warrant legal intervention. Speech which is not likely to culminate in this way does not warrant such intervention.

The risk which is created in the sedition offences is that mere teaching and advocacy are wide enough and vague enough concepts to encompass the soapbox orator who has no followers and the intellectual theoretician who seeks no followers. A person who expresses the desirability of over-throwing the government by force is not necessarily a threat. A person who intellectually justifies revolution or violence is not necessarily a threat. The threat is the call to action by someone who has followers. The law properly intervenes at the point where speech is likely to precipitate immediate action. Therefore, the sedition sections should prohibit not the mere teaching or advocacy of the violent overthrow of govern-ment, but rather the *incitement* to such action. In the poli-tically polarized climate that we have created, we run the risk of punishing the impotent preacher along with the dangerous demagogue. The Criminal Code should be amended to confine the offence of sedition to the incitement of violence against Government in situations where there is a clear and present danger that the incitement will be acted on.

Causing a Disturbance and Unlawful Assembly

In the summer of 1969, a young man was convicted of the offence of "causing a disturbance" for shouting "traitor Tru-deau" at a Liberal Party picnic. Why was it an offence to shout nasty slogans at a noisy picnic? Of course, if a person were to shout even messages of brotherhood so as effectively to interfere with the rights of others, such behaviour might be legitimately punishable. For example, there is no need to tolerate such voluminous vocal ventilation at an otherwise orderly meeting or on a residential street at four o'clock in the morning. Moreover, there might be some basis for visit-ing penal consequences on the person who shouts a sustained barrage of insults and invective at private citizens. But why, if the target is the Prime Minister and other *public* decision-makers in a noisy public place? Shouldn't the law require that their tolerance be higher?

It appears that the disturbance in question was "caused" by the fact that the slogan was so unpopular in that particular milieu that the supporters of the Prime Minister were pro-voked to a physical attack upon the accused. Clearly, if the accused had shouted "Bravo Trudeau" no disturbance would have been "caused". The gist of this offence seems to be that the utterances of the speaker attracted violence to himself. Some of the old cases dealing with "unlawful assembly" appear also to take a similar line.

Regrettably, the foregoing case may be a valid expression of the present state of the law. In an article dealing with recent amendments to the offence of "causing a disturbance" one eminent legal authority, Dr. Mark MacGuigan made the following comment:

In my opinion these words change the traditional law . . . and create an offence . . . where someone uses insulting language in or near a public place and a disturbance results, even without any intention on the part of the speaker to provoke a breach of the peace.

It is not difficult to foresee the infinite possibilities for repression which inhere in this offence. To whatever extent the law remains in its present form, we will be permitting a violent heckler to exercise an effective veto on freedom of speech and assembly. This section should be amended in order to make clear that, in the context of political and social controversy, a person will be punished not for attracting the violence of antagonists to himself, but rather for inciting the violence of his followers against others.

Hate Propaganda

Recently, a new substantive offence has been added to the Criminal Code. In an effort to counteract a slight resurgence of neo-Nazi activity, Parliament has made it illegal to communicate statements which willfully promote hatred against people because of race, religion, and ethnicity. But many useful utterances in a democratic society will promote what could be described, at the very least, as bitter feelings. The dividing line between creative tension and destructive hate will often be very difficult to draw. Moreover, in its present form, the enactment might imperil people who bear no remote resemblance to the Nazi element for which it was intended.

For example, if a French Canadian nationalist were to denounce the English Canadians for the alleged exploitation of French Canada, could it be said that he was willfully promoting "hatred" of English speaking Canadians? If an Indian were to heap the blame for his poverty upon the white man, could he be said to be willfully promoting "hatred" for white people? If a Jew were to indict all of Germany for the atrocities of the Nazis, could he be accused of wilfully promoting "hatred" against all Germans?

Whether or not one agrees with the kinds of views which these people express in the foregoing examples, it would be unfair, unwise, and undemocratic to make them illegal. Yet we run the risk that the formulation, "willfully promote hatred", could lead to precisely such results.

Moreover, the defences which are provided in this section may not be adequate to protect many legitimate exercises of free speech. The defence of truth will have very little application in view of the fact that most utterances in the political arena deal with opinion rather than fact. The immunity conferred upon subjects of "public interest" gives to the courts far too much power to set the framework of democratic political polemics. On the basis of what criteria and in the light of what evidence will the courts determine whether a matter is in the "public interest"?

In my view, the risk which this enactment creates to the free speech of a wide variety of people is not justified by the evidence of trouble or potential trouble to the victims of hate propaganda. The Cohen Committee itself, which recommended this legislation, admitted that the hate mongering problem in Canada cannot be described "as one of crisis or near crisis proportion". Moreover, the Director of the Ontario Human Rights Commission, one of the most active government bodies in the field of race relations, declared that ". . . the Canadian public is relatively immune to extremist, anti-semitic and other 'hate' materials."

In view of the minimal risk to the well being of the intended victims of Nazi propaganda and the potential risk to the free speech of those who have no connection with Nazi propaganda, the best course would be the complete repeal of this section.

Scandalizing Contempt of Court

In the spring of 1969, a young student in the Maritimes went to jail for having written in a university student publication that a certain trial was a "mockery of justice" and that the courts were "tools of the corporate elite". The offence?

Scandalizing the court and particularly the presiding judge by bringing the court, the judge, and the proceedings in the trial into "public ridicule and contempt".

A few years earlier, a Vancouver newspaper writer was convicted of scandalizing contempt of court for a crusading article which he had written against the use of capital punishment. In the article he described the jury in a particular capital trial as "the people who planned the murder" of the convicted man and the judge as the one who "chose the time and place and caused the victim to suffer the exquisite torture of anticipation".

What social purpose was served by the imposition of criminal punishment for the exercise of such speech? The offence of scandalizing contempt of court was designed to protect the administration of justice. According to the theory, the courts could not function without the respect of the community. Public statements which lowered or tended to lower public esteem for the courts could undermine judicial authority

In my view, this is a piece of fatuous mythology. What about the administrative tribunals which also dispense important justice? They can claim no analagous protection to their social reputations. Yet no one has seriously suggested that the Municipal Board, the Liquor Control Board, the C.R.T.C., or the Labour Relations Board need such immunity from contemptuous public criticism. Moreover, the United States Supreme Court, which has no comparable power, has sustained much more vicious attacks without diminution of its eminent role in American society.

On the other hand, an atmosphere of vigorous criticism could improve the quality of judicial performance. Moreover, as the courts move increasingly to the centre of our bitterest social controversies, the right of unfettered criticism will provide an important outlet for disaffected litigants.

The mere existence of the power to punish for scandalizing contempt will serve to inhibit critical commentary. Indeed, the layman who wishes to criticize will be unable to determine in advance whether his proposed remarks are likely to be impugned. The lawyer who wishes to advise him intelligently will be forced to err on the side of caution. Regrettably, the cases reveal little consistency as to what kind of statements will constitute contempt. What one judge may find contemptuous, another may consider fair comment. Compare, for example, the statements which were found contemptous in the foregoing cases with the following:

> Mr. Saint Aubyn is reducing the judicial character to the level of a clown.

> . . . Mr. Justice Higgins is, we believe, what is called a political judge, that is he was appointed because he had well served a political party. He, moreover, seems to know his position, and does not mean to allow any reflection on those to whom he may be said to be in debt for his judgeship.

In both of these cases, the courts acquitted the writers of scandalizing contempt of court. On what basis can we say that the remarks in these cases were any less contemptuous than the ones quoted earlier?

It is better that the judges earn respect through the quality of justice which they dispense rather than through the threat of punishment they can impose. The offence of contempt of court could well be preserved to punish rowdy behaviour in the courtroom, violations of court orders, and commentaries outside of court which would prejudice the interests of litigants before the courts. But there is no basis whatever for perpetuating the power to punish out of court commentary that allegedly "scandalizes" the courts.

A judge injured by malicious and false statements should have no more power to vindicate his interests than what is available to the ordinary citizen – an action for damages.

Defamatory Libel

During the winter of 1969, a young man in British Columbia was convicted of "defamatory libel" for writing an article in an underground newspaper which awarded "the Pontius Pilate certificate" to a Vancouver magistrate. This case resurrected the offence of defamatory libel from the grave of obscurity in which it had been resting for a generation. It inflicts the punishment of the criminal law upon a person for making a statement that is "likely to injure the reputation of any person by exposing him to hatred, contempt, or ridicule". The original rationale for this offence grew out of the danger that "libellous" statements could provoke breaches of the peace. By now, however, the Criminal Code is overflowing with offences which incite or tend to incite breaches of the peace. In this connection consider the following: counselling the commission of an offence, attempting to commit an offence, causing a disturbance, watching and besetting, obstructing, etc. In view of the multiplicity of prohibitions against promoting breaches of the peace, there is very little role for defamatory libel to play in that area. Virtually the only remaining role is the protection of injured reputations. But why should there be *prosecutions* to vindicate reputations? Why does the state have a greater interest in the reputation of 'A' than in the free speech of 'B'? It is one thing for 'A' to launch a civil action for damages in order to redress the libellous statements of 'B'. But it is quite another matter to threaten 'B' with prosecution, conviction, and possible imprisonment. The vindication of personal reputation does not warrant the awesome power of incarceration. This offence constitutes an additional peril to freedom of speech which cannot be justified by an overriding social value.

Parade By-laws

In the fall of 1968, a group of Vietnam War demonstrators sought a parade permit to march down Toronto's busy Yonge Street. Instead, they were offered a permit to march down Bay Street and University Avenue. Unfortunately, on Saturdays, Bay Street and University Avenue are virtually urban deserts. Thus the parade threatened to become not an exercise in free speech but an exercise in free soliloquy.

Where the Criminal Code usually punishes unlawful speech *after* it has occurred, local by-laws can effectively inhibit speech *before* it occurs. Police authorities exert a peculiar power over freedom of speech and assembly. In virtually every major municipality in this country, the chief of police or police commission has been given the power to determine the time and the route of parades and demonstrations. The determination of time and route is no routine act. It can affect the potency of a demonstration.

Consider this example. The Metropolitan Toronto Police Commission has enacted a by-law which prohibits parades and demonstrations on busy streets unless the parade has been occuring annually for ten consecutive years prior to October 1st, 1964. This exception protects the Santa Claus parade. But the Santa Claus parade is one event which does not require a busy street for an audience. Crowds will flock to whatever street might be assigned to this annual ritual.

On the other hand, political protest could be rendered virtually impotent without ready access to a busy street and an available audience. Without a large audience, it might very well lack the newsworthiness even to attract attention from the media. Herein lies the subtlety of our problem. In Canada we don't ban demonstrations, we re-route them.

The Metropolitan Police by-law also provides that exceptions might be made and busy street parade permits might be granted under "unusual circumstances of municipal, provincial or federal importance". But the power to determine what qualifies as an "unusual circumstance" is exercised by the Chairman of the Police Commission and the chief of police.

A little research will uncover a host of "unusual circumstances" in which these police officials have granted the right to parade on Toronto's busy Yonge Street. Among such exceptions was a convention of the racially segregated Fraternal Order of Eagles. Although this group was granted the permit it sought, the Vietnam parade was re-routed from the busy portions of Yonge Street.

The Metro police by-law would appear to provide a most feeble basis for the exercise of so basic a democratic right as freedom of assembly — feeble because of its perennial priority for freedom of traffic over freedom of assembly, feeble because it considers social ritual more important than political protest, and feeble because it delegates the power to make exceptions to police officials. Granted, political protesters cannot be given automatic access to any street at any time. But the crucial power to set out the criteria for determining time and place should be given to an elected body not to an appointed one.

The crucial power to apply those criteria in particular cases should be given to someone other than a police body. The police interest in a demonstration is an orderly flow of traffic; the demonstrator's interest is a conspicuous event. Often, these interests are in conflict. No law or by-law should make the police umpires of their own ball game. Yet the by-laws of virtually every major municipality in this country give to the police such amazing power. By re-routing and re-scheduling,

110

they can take the life out of protest. The preservation of such power in the hands of the police constitutes an unwarranted impediment to the right of non-violent dissent.

Beyond Freedom of Speech

As important as freedom of speech is, it is not an adequate instrument for promoting social change. Freedom of speech is based upon the questionable proposition that people can be persuaded by rational argument. Unfortunately, this is a fallacious description of human behaviour. A social order which confines social protest to rational debate would load the dice against social change. Pressure, not reason, is the chief instrument of social persuasion. An employer who pays low wages is more likely to be moved by a well-organized strike than by a well-prepared sermon. Politicians hungering for position will respond more to political tension than to logical syllogism.

This is not to advocate the abandonment of reason in our social discourse. It is to recognize its limitations. Granted pressure without reason is irresponsible, but reason without pressure is ineffectual. Of course, the range of pressure may not include physical violence. Violence is too much and reason is not enough. The proper operation of the democratic processes demands the effective right to exert non-violent and unpleasant pressures.

Social reformers will need to exert these pressures not only against government, but also against other institutions, both public and private. Social change can be effected not only by the decisions of government, but also by the actions of employers, landlords, educators, etc. What our new era will require is a set of fair ground rules for the waging of inter-citizen and inter-group conflict. The role of the law is to distribute the levers of pressure more equitably among the parties to social conflict. The more advantaged parties use money as their primary instrument of pressure. The less advantaged use their bodies – they can organize pressure groups, create picket lines, conduct boycotts and so on. Unfortunately in to-day's Canada, the ground rules are not working fairly. The instruments of pressure available to the less advantaged are beset with legal impediments.

Where the street demonstration is usually addressed to broad issues of public policy, the picket line usually zeroes in on special issues of business policy. Picket lines are set up near business establishments in order to pressure the proprietor to change his policy. The idea is to discourage customer patronage and employee recruitment until improvements are made. The picket line is one of the most potent weapons of non-violent pressure for workers against employers and for buyers against sellers. No nation committed to the rhetoric of democracy would dare to abolish the right to picket for a lawful purpose. We are more ingenious. In most provinces in this country, we don't abolish picket lines, we cut them down. Evidence of violence or disorder on a picket line can produce a court injunction restricting the number of pickets to not more than three or four per gate. What may have begun as a powerful expression of vital grievances will end up looking like a pathetic advertisement for "Eat at Joe's".

The restrictive injunction confines the pickets to rational discussion. The pickets are solemnly reminded that the token picket line has preserved for them the right to disseminate information about their dispute. They are told they don't need large numbers to convey information. True. But how in the world will the mere dissemination of information help the pickets to persuade prospective employees and customers to stay away from the impugned establishment? Self-interest propels people to continue dealing with the proprietor. They go there seeking economic benefit. How can a token picket line compete with that?

Of course, we cannot allow the pickets to employ violence. But it would be unfair to confine them to reason. The picket line which is both justified and effective will exert social pressure on those seeking access to the picketed premises. The idea is to visit the collective contempt of the protesters on those who would cross the picket line. The object is to make the "scab" feel capable of standing up under a worm every time he enters the impugned premises. This is the discomfort which the pickets must inflict in order to offset the benefits which the proprietor can offer.

The reduced picket line necessarily weakens the pickets' ability to heap social pressure upon a person who would enter the impugned premises. A large demonstration carries greater moral weight in our community than does a token one. Token picketing, regardless of the realities, tends to convey an appearance of half-hearted or non-existent support. If the proprietor may attempt to entice people through his doors with economic benefit, why can't the pickets attempt to repel them with social pressure?

The aim should be equality of bargaining power. Clearly, the restrictive injunction unduly favours proprietors against protesters. Social peace and public order are the interests most invariably invoked to justify picket line restrictions. This raises the dubious proposition that because 'X' commits violence on a picket line, 'Y' can be prohibited from picketing. If 'X' commits violence, 'X' should be charged and convicted. But 'Y' should not be denied one of his few effective weapons of non-violent pressure.

In most situations, there is no reason to doubt the ability of the police to protect the public peace even in a setting of large picket line demonstrations. Not long ago, for example, the Montreal police department was credited with having performed magnificently in protecting the peace during the controversial McGill-français march. That was a march of five thousand. The largest picket line is rarely a fraction of that. Only in those rare circumstances where it can be reasonably demonstrated that police power is not sufficient to protect the peace should there be any consideration given to interfering with picket line activity. When we reduce the size, we remove the sting.

The Right to Boycott

Another instrument of non-violent pressure for change is the consumer boycott. This tactic involves the collective withdrawal of financial patronage from an institution whose policies are under attack. Properly organized, the boycott can be a potent weapon. Very few injuries can elicit the response of financial injury. The Negroes of Montgomery Alabama repealed one hundred years of segregation by collectively depriving the bus company of their customary patronage. The United Farm Workers won collective bargaining

113

rights through a nation-wide boycott of California grapes.

The problem is that a boycott is very difficult to organize. It is an attempt to sell an amorphous mass of people on the legitimacy of a cause. Apart from the economic difficulties in organization, the conduct of a consumer boycott is beset with legal obstacles. Unless they have enormous resources in order to undertake an advertising campaign, the boycotters will probably seek to publicize their appeal at the very places where the products of the impugned establishment are being offered for public sale. Very often this will lead to picket lines in front of retail outlets which are not parties to the central dispute.

The difficulty is that in almost every jurisdiction in this country the proprietor of a picketed establishment in these circumstances could probably secure a court injunction to prohibit *all* of the picketing near his premises. When people involved in a dispute with one party picket the premises of another party, such activity is considered "secondary picketing" and may, therefore, be liable to complete prohibition.

A few years ago a clothing workers' union decided to launch a boycott against their employer's product. Some of the products were being sold at a retail store in a small Ontario community. The union set up a small picket line in front of the store; their signs simply identified the goods in question and declared that they were not union made. There was no attempt to discourage general public patronage of the retail establishment. The proprietor of the store sought and secured a court injunction removing all of the pickets from the vicinity of his premises. The Ontario Court of Appeal declared that ". . . the right . . . to engage in secondary picketing . . . must give way to (a business man's) right to trade. . .". Through judicial pronouncement and in some cases legislation, such secondary picketing is prohibitable almost everywhere in Canada. Conceivably, this doctrine might apply even outside the labour context in which it was spawned.

Why is the right of the merchant to trade more holy than the right of the boycotter to engage in secondary picketing? Significantly, the pickets could not *force* the public to boycott the premises or the goods. All they can do is attempt to *persuade* the public to boycott the goods. As long as the objective of the boycott is not unlawful, why shouldn't the public be able to choose for itself between the salesmanship of the proprietor and the appeals of the pickets?

Of course, some boycotts have been and will continue to be inequitable and unreasonable. But, unless their goals are unlawful, it is better to let the consuming public make the decision. The public, not the courts, should decide whether to support the seller or the boycotter and whether the cause is more valuable than the product. Such an approach, at least, maximizes freedom of choice. It enables the less advantaged to compete more equally with the more advantaged. The law should referee the conflict, not determine its outcome.

The Right to Retaliate

Several months ago in a Canadian city, a notice was served on two tenants requiring them to vacate their apartments by the end of the month. Coincidentally, they had just organized a union of tenants and had successfully secured a reduction in rent from a recalcitrant landlord. At the beginning of the 1970 school season, two high school students in a Canadian city were ordered by the Board of Education to transfer to another school. Both of them had been involved in the publication and dissemination throughout their school of a newspaper highly critical of some of their teachers.

Pressure invites retaliation. We cannot deny the recipient of pressure the right to retaliate with pressure. The concern of the law should not be who wins the fight but how the fight is waged. The ground rules must be fair. However, some types of retaliation exceed the limits of fairness. This may occur when one party has the power unilaterally to deny his adversary the necessities of life – job, home, education. Only the superheroic would take such risks. Since society is composed essentially of men rather than of saints, such retaliatory power can render academic our instruments of non-violent pressure.

The instruments of non-violent pressure must enjoy some immunity against excessive retaliation. This will explain some of the changes in our labour relations legislation. At one time employers could punish union membership with loss of employment. Clearly, the existence of the right to join unions became less than meaningful when the employer could so punish its exercise. To-day our labour laws prohibit discrimination for union activity and they empower independent tribunals to reinstate and compensate for such violations.

What we have done to protect employment, we must do for other day-to-day activities. Consider the landlord-tenant relationship. Apartment tenants all over Canada are banding together to exert greater pressure and engage in collective bargaining with their landlords. Of course, they have the legal right to create such organizations. But numbers of landlords have threatened organizers and members with eviction. In some cases, they have even carried out the threat. Tenant union organizers report that scores of people have refused to join because of the fear of retaliatory eviction.

In such a situation, the democratic right to form tenant pressure groups is somewhat illusory. For too many people the loss of home will be too great a price to pay for the exercise of this right. At the very least, legislation should remove from landlords the power to retaliate against tenants simply because they joined tenant organizations. Moreover, we should make available impartial and expeditious machinery with the power to rescind evictions which are held to be retaliatory.

Another example of such power exists in the relationship between students and educational authorities. On campuses and in high schools all over the country, students are challenging the policies of educational authorities. The inequity arises from the fact that in most cases the educational authority has the legal power to suspend and expel. Although this is not the place to set out the limits of permissible pressure for students, it is the place to call for due process in campus conflicts. Since the education authority is an interested party in disputes with rebelling students, it should not have the final say. It should not be empowered unilaterally to deprive a person of his education. The student should be entitled to appeal suspensions and expulsions to impartial and independent adjudication.

Our various instruments of non-violent pressure must not only be permitted, they must also be protected. They cannot effectively co-exist with the unilateral power to deny the necessities of life. At the very least, we should modify the unilateral feature. We should provide impartial adjudication for denial of residence and education as we have for denial of employment.

* * *

The invocation of emergency powers has dangerously polarized Canadian society. The conduct of the crisis has sustained the impression that the citizen has no choice except insurrection or repression. Muddle-headed leftists are defending illegitimate violence; right wing yahoos are attacking legitimate non-violence.

The post-crisis survival of Canadian democracy requires the expansion of effective alternatives. The aggrieved and the disaffected must have more viable channels of non-violent expression – in speech, assembly, economic sanction, and organization. One need not side with rebels against authority, labour against management, tenants against landlords, students against educators, or consumers against producers in order to challenge the present law and the present ground rules. One simply needs a sense of fair play and a desire to make democracy work. Which side is right or wrong at any particular time is not the primary concern of the law in this context. The concern of the law here should be that all parties, right or wrong, have the effective opportunity to impress their views on the social consensus.

It is in this direction that we might find an alternative to the unacceptable extremes of the polarized society. The concept of civil liberties was never more relevant.

Québec and Canadian Nationalism: Two Views

Abraham Rotstein

Abraham Rotstein was educated at McGill (B.A.), the University of Chicago, Columbia, and the University of Toronto (Ph.D.). At present he is an Associate Professor of Economics at the University of Toronto. He is also the founding member of the University League for Social Reform, Managing Editor of the *Canadian Forum*, editor of *The Prospect of Change* and *Proposals for Canada's Future*, and member of the Task Force on the Structure of Industry and the Role of Foreign Ownership (Watkins Report). He has written numerous articles on foreign investment in Canada and on Canadian nationalism.

Gad Horowitz

Mr. Horowitz is thirty-four years old. He is a Political Scientist, formerly at McGill and now at the University of Toronto. He is Associate Editor of *Canadian Dimension* and author of *Canadian Labour in Politics*.

Quebec and Canadian nationalism: two views

ABRAHAM ROTSTEIN
GAD HOROWITZ

As the shock of the recent crisis begins to lift, we are tempted, each of us, to find some vindication of our personal position in the events that have shaken this country to the core. Nationalists, liberals, federalists and separatists will be inclined to bring their own traditional interpretation to these events. Such a process, faithfully pursued, can only recreate the underlying conditions of the crisis and its related consequences – another round of violence followed by yet stronger repression. Since the only option available to us is to change ourselves, we must begin at the point where each of us stands.

* * *

Looking back on the fragile plant called English Canadian nationalism, I feel that our broad analysis of the situation of Canada as a whole can be re-affirmed, while our position on Quebec has proved weak and illusory. One must say at the outset, of course, that there are as many varieties of nationalism, even in English Canada, as there are social philosophies. In a position that I have attempted to define as "the nationalism of the left", our emphasis has been on the retention and the regaining of the crucial powers of decision in this country in the many realms of economic, social and cultural life. At stake is the integrity of the apparatus of the nation-state as a means for implementing the growing number of tasks assigned to it by its citizens, from mass education through social welfare and full employment. The nation-state is particularly important as a social counterforce to the spreading technological society in easing its disruptive costs and distributing more equally its benefits. In an age of rapidly spreading global corporations, only the nation-state remains as a regulatory power and safeguard of sufficient strength against the vast reorganization of resources and global planning carried on by these corporations in their own interests.

The underlying premises of such a position rest on a recognition of the realities of power in the modern world and the shared values and common interests of collectivities in directing that power to common purposes. In that sense, such a position stands opposed to the atomized individualism of the liberal view of society with its faith in the benevolence of blind market forces.

Recognition, however, of a separate community in Quebec, of an indigenous collectivity seeking many of the same powers of decision for itself as we sought for Canada as a whole, lacked a clear definition in this scheme. The logic of the argument halted when it moved from the plane of moral recognition to political implementation. By waiting, we hoped eventually for a joint political solution to common problems. In this regard however, nationalists of English Canada could not proceed beyond some of their colleagues in Quebec engaged in the same search. Thus the support of the process of self-determination for Quebec was from a distance. Many of us sincerely held the view that once Quebec had arrived at a consensus on its own course of action, we would be prepared to support it. Implicitly at least, we felt that the lethargy and indifference in English Canada to the issue would never bring us to use troops if Quebec should decide to separate.

But the irony of history is supreme. Could we ever have imagined that the leading convert in this country to Lord Acton and to Manchester liberalism would be the architect of unprecedented repression? Could we have foreseen that the prophet of nineteenth century individualism would flex the political contours of our nation-state in a way that has never happened before, creating a national unity through fear and an almost limitless craving among the people for authority, for troops and for police?

Mr. Trudeau has been given undue credit for "flexibility" and for his ability to adapt his philosophy to "circumstances". In reality, the road from Manchester liberalism to the repressive state leads in a straight line. The illusions of Lord Acton that centre on the non-recognition of power must in the end rediscover this reality with a vengeance and devoid of moderation. One example will suffice. American extraterritorial jurisdiction in this country that has accompanied American foreign investment has increasingly eroded Canadian sovereignty over a long period. Yet the Prime Minister has never concerned himself seriously with this manifestation of American "parallel power". It is a problem which has moderate and viable solutions, as the Watkins Report has demonstrated. Instead, the issue of "parallel power" emerges full-blown as if it had never existed before the FLQ, and is dealt with through a national hysteria of political and military overkill. Thus our own totalitarianism – the ultimate warning of liberals to nationalists – turns out to be founded in that tissue of shallow ninteenth century fictions about man and society which liberals regard as their ideal. Unable to recognize the legitimate demands of community and the integrity of the institutions of power that nationalists advocate, liberals become thereby the chief architects of the repressive society in a crisis. As their ideals collapse, their refuge in the apparatus of the state is uncritical and untempered.

Since the concrete powers of the War Measures Act. and the Public Order Act have been almost no help whatever in meeting the criminal challenge of the FLQ, only their symbolic function will explain their implementation and their popularity. While that symbolism is far from being clear, it is a cry in the liberal void – the traumatic discovery that power, authority and the state are the realities of our national life and that we will have unlimited and uncritical affirmation of these symbols in a crisis. The costs of the sudden transition from illusion to reality are almost limitless and are willingly borne by frightened liberals.

* * *

It is still too early to draw more than an interim balance sheet. Nationalists in English Canada must face up to their own illusions about Quebec and change their position accordingly. The chief of these is the sentimental reverie that Quebec's separation could be painless and passive if sufficient goodwill and understanding could be brought to bear on both sides. If Quebec nationalists have given little thought to the political strategy of recreating their political framework, English-Canadian nationalists have offered little more than an empty goodwill and benevolence. The events of the past few months can be read in many ways. I draw my own lesson from the fact that English and French Canada appear, unexpectedly, to be interlocked and mutually interwoven in a way that permits no such easy restructuring of the status quo without an immense and complex political effort on both sides.

Some may prefer to cling to an old scenario. If Lévesque and the Parti Québecois had won the last election, would we not have acceded to separation with ease and good grace? It is a tantalizing question and now totally irrelevant. The opportunity may have existed on a single occasion but it has now vanished. The frustrations that produced the moral climate in which the FLQ emerged are now magnified and doubly embittered. The War Measures Act and the deployment of troops have created a precedent that will be more easily invoked a second time. Together they have shifted the modalities of our politics from parliamentary electioneering to a range of confrontations, of semi-legal and illegal initiatives which will become the order of the day. Too many new forces have been unleashed, too many old resentments have been sharpened and projected onto the scene, too many appetites whetted for violence (both governmental and guerilla), to write a peaceful scenario any more. Our politics have moved beyond the constitutional debates and the self-indulgent literary anguish of the two-solitudes epoch. A neanderthal addiction to force has surfaced and only a supreme romantic will expect our politics to retreat into the channels prescribed by Westminister code books. Our Prime Minister promised initially to root out the cancer, so-called, of this violence only to be contradicted several weeks later by M. Bourassa who explained, quite properly, that it could not be done. Meantime, how are we to regard Mr. Trudeau's long-term strategy and techniques of polarization other than as an escalation beyond the realm of the normal political process of consensus and accommodation?

In a word, the modalities of our politics have shifted and we should abandon the vain hope that violence will suddenly destroy itself and that its heritage will evaporate.

Nationalists in English Canada can only regard this escalation with the deepest pessimism. We have introduced into the realm of legitimacy, and indeed probability, the use of military force and emergency powers to achieve *political* ends. As events run their course along the new incidents of semi-legal and illegal outbursts and responses, we will travel thereby the highway towards the ultimate resolution of Quebec's separation. The costs of Quebec remaining within Confederation may be as high as those of separating. We shall all pay heavily, whatever the outcome.

Quebec nationalists, of whatever persuasion, must now

recognize in the circumstances that they cannot achieve their objectives at any reasonable cost without active support from English Canadians. Nationalists in the rest of the country must realize that the continued repression of Quebec will only create a society which is not worth inhabiting.

Our mutual interests must be recognized. The old empathy and passive moral support are no longer sufficient. We must now travel in tandem to create in English Canada active legal, political and institutional channels that support and foster Quebec's legitimate aspirations. It is our only hope of mitigating the impact of the collision which looms ahead.

Our dialogue must be reopened in a serious rather than a sentimental vein; our emphasis must be on techniques, on institutions, and strategies that deal evenhandedly with the interests of two emerging nations. But no one can be optimistic about the future.

ABRAHAM ROTSTEIN

Three years ago – ages ago – I participated in a Le Devoir symposium on "Quebec in the Canada of Tomorrow". I was one of those advocating a special status for Quebec. My main argument was that a loosening of the federal bond was essential for the survival of a healthy *English*-Canadian collectivity:

> In large part, the weakness of the English Canadian community results from the fact that its national state also serves as that of the French Canadians (who) insist that (it) . . . must never . . . become so powerful that the autonomy of Quebec is threatened. The result is that Ottawa does not have sufficient power . . . to integrate the diverse tribes, provinces and regions of English-speaking Canada. And disintegration opens the door to Americanization. Special status for Quebec is the only way to break out of the present trap which offers us a choice only between imposing centralization on Quebec and imposing decentralization on the rest of Canada.

Today it is clear that the perpetuation of the arrangement of 1867 threatens not only the *épanouissement* – the development, the vigour, the forward movement – of both peoples, but their essential character as relatively free societies committed to individual liberty, parliamentary democracy, and peaceful change. But English Canadians still have no leaders interested in *their* welfare as a community who will take the necessary initiatives on *their* behalf towards a radical restructuring of the Canada-Quebec relationship.

The elites of Quebec are very badly divided. The separatists, increasingly alienated, are on the point of denying the very legitimacy of the regime. The federalists, increasingly hysterical, are prepared to use the most repressive methods in order to exorcize subversive demons. *The Prime Minister of Canada is the leader of one of the factions in this incipient Quebec civil war.* The ignorance, the prejudice, the economic and military power of English Canadians are for him essentially resources to be used against his enemies in Quebec. If English Canadian democracy as well as Quebec democracy must therefore perish in the struggle. . .

Well, here we are, Christmas 1970. It is so much worse than we thought possible. It will get much worse still, unless English Canada can find its Lévesque.

GAD HOROWITZ

The CANADIAN FORUM is one of the oldest continuously published monthly magazines in Canada. Originally styled "A Monthly Journal of Literature and Public Affairs," and more recently "An Independent Journal of Opinion and the Arts," the FORUM features political and social commentary on current Canadian problems as well as literature and poetry by Canadian authors. It is a noncommercial publication financed by readers' subscriptions.

Recent newspaper comments on the FORUM include the following:

"variety and incisiveness"
  Ottawa Citizen

"un sérieux remarquable"
  Claude Ryan in *Le Devoir*

"able and interesting articles . . . . the one journal that will publish material too difficult, or too scandalous for commercial magazines."
  Kildare Dobbs in *Toronto Daily Star*

"probably the best-looking non-glossy around. Very clean, good line drawings, good horizontal design."
  Marq de Villiers in the *Telegram*

Annual subscription ($5.00) are available from the

CANADIAN FORUM LIMITED
56 Esplande Street East,
Toronto 1

The Quebec issue of *The Canadian Forum* on the October Crisis sold out immediately on hitting the news-stands last January. Published now by *new press*, in permanent form and with photographs and a new Postscript, *Power Corrupted* is a collection of articles which have already drawn wide comment.

The authors of *Power Corrupted* have taken as their point of departure, a sincere concern to understand the Quebec unrest . . . They have been brought back, by the logic of an honest search, to a central question which obliges them to ask anew what are the sources of their own identity.

. . . If the foremost effect of the October crisis in English Canada, was to be the abandoning, once and for all of the fruitless approach of false paternalism and instead was to raise the problem of English Canada's very existence, the chances of a genuine encounter would be increased. For at the crucial level of their own existence, the two peoples who make up Canada have much more to say to one another and have much more in common than they have been willing to acknowledge hitherto.

Claude Ryan

The War Measures crisis of October, 1970, when this nation was caught between the violent demands of fanatical men and the repressive responses of our federal politicians, marked a water shed in our history — a time that tried the consciences and exacerbated the emotions of Canadians everywhere. *Power Corrupted* brilliantly distills the issues, the feelings and the fears that caused Canada to declare a state of war in a time of peace.

Peter C. Newman

COVER PHOTO
Toronto Star &
Miller Services, Toronto